FOURTH INDIAN REFLECTIONS

MEMOIRS OF A GREAT COMPANY

COMPILED BY

DENIS BLOMFIELD-SMITH

PRIVATELY PRINTED

1987

Fourth Indian Reflections may be obtained from
Brigadier D. C. Blomfield-Smith, The Abbey,
Cockfield, Bury St. Edmunds, Suffolk IP30 0LB

Printed in England by Larman Printers, Cambridge

(ii)

"For the fame of this Division will surely go down as one of the greatest fighting formations in military history: to be spoken of with such as the Tenth Legion, The Light Division of the Peninsular War, Napoleon's Old Guard".

"Those who fought under the sign of the Red Eagle will always be justly proud of it; and those commanders who, like myself have known the worth in the field of that magnificent Division, will be the first to acknowledge their debt of gratitude, and to salute one of the greatest bands of fighting men who have ever served together in this troubled world of wars and warriors".

FIELD MARSHAL LORD WAVELL in 1948
in his Foreword to
The History of the 4th Indian Division.

Preface

The inspiration for this collection of reminiscences originated from Colonel C. A. H. M. Noble, MC, late of 2nd Camerons and presently President of the 4th Indian Division (1939/47) Officer's Association. The book attempts to reflect the unique qualities of a great company of men. At this late stage this is a truly daunting task because so many of that company who may have survived the years of combat have since succumbed to the passage of years: also memories, even of events that are unforgettable, have dimmed as regards detail. However, true to the tradition of a fighting formation which never flinched from the apparently impossible, here is our attempt. The passages in italics are included in order to set the scene. It is hoped that those who certainly do not need them, will tolerate them for the sake of those who do: remembering that, sadly, the numbers who will read these reflections, and who were there, are becoming fewer. Those who look for historical detail should read the Divisional history. The history that is recorded here is that created by unquenchable spirit.

Grateful acknowledgement is made to the following, whose contributions are included or who have helped so much in other ways.: Major-General D. A. Beckett CB DSO: Major R. J. Henderson: Lieut-Colonel J. F. B. Huntley MC: Major F. R. Jephson MC: Lieut-Colonel H. M. A. Knight MC: Brigadier H. W. D. McDonald DSO: Major E. Morrow: Major R. A. Perkin MC: Brigadier H. W. Picken OBE: Lieut-Colonel P. A. R. Reyne OBE MC: Brigadier I. A. Roche DSO: Lieut-General Sir Reginald Savory KCIE CB DSO MC: Major G. P. Smart MC: Major T. Tait MBE: Major C. W. Windle MC: Lieut-Colonel E. J. Wyld MC. Finally, I wish to record the great contribution of the history of the Division – "Fourth Indian Division" by Lieutenant-Colonel G. R. Stevens OBE (published by McLaren & Son Ltd) – not only to this book but, more importantly, to the memories of those privileged to serve in such peerless company.

D. C. BLOMFIELD-SMITH
Editor

THE START POINT

The Predator which Changed its Prey

In Southern India in 1935 the mobilisation role of Deccan District was to provide two Infantry Brigades for despatch overseas. Scheme HERON was the plan for sending 11th (Ahmednagar) Infantry Brigade to Egypt and scheme EMU involved the despatch of 12th (Secunderabad) Infantry Brigade to Malaya. The formation which was to provide the framework to hold these brigades was to be 4th Indian Division. By 1939 Scheme HERON had evolved so that the force earmarked for Egypt had become HQ 4th Indian Division and 11th Infantry Brigade from Deccan District and 5th (Jhansi) Infantry Brigade.

In May 1939 Major-General the Hon P. G. Scarlett, MC, Commander-designate of 4th Indian Division attended a conference in Egypt to discuss the movement and employment of Indian troops in the Middle East; including the possibility of movement overland, should the Italians prevent movement through the Red Sea.

In the words of the history of 4th Indian Division:

"On July 31st, Brigadier A. B. McPherson, MVO, MC, led out 2 Cameron Highlanders (Lieut-Col. A. Anderson, MC), 1/6 Rajputana Rifles (Lieut-Col. L. S. Bell-Syer), 4/7 Rajput Regiment (Lieut-Col. A. B. Blaxland) and 4 Field Regiment R.A. (Lieut-Col. L. F. Thompson, MC) – the original units of 11 Indian Infantry Brigade Group. On August 2nd, three transports sailed from Bombay. Eleven days later through the shimmering heat, the sepoys saw the desolate Egyptian ridges closing up on one bow, the bleak Sinai wastes on the other. Next morning the transports dropped anchor in Port Tewfik. Within a few hours the Brigade Group had settled under canvas at Fayid Camp.

Four hundred miles to the west of the Nile, in their camps along the Libyan frontier, the Italian garrisons continued to saunter through their customary routines. On September 19th an advance reconnaissance party from 11 Brigade proceeded to Western Desert. They took the

1

road so many came to know so well, turning north at the Pyramids across a hundred miles of hard sand to the causeway over the magenta lagoons behind Alexandria, thence west through the rolling dunes which skirted the bright thunderous Mediterranean, past scattered date oases and fig plantations until beyond the dusty hamlet of Burgh el Arab the road rose to the crest of the dunes and along the easy valley inland a train snorted up to a sun-bitten drought-stricken halt whose name, (which did not matter then), was El Alamein".

The order of battle of the Division at this time was:

Divisional Cavalry Regiment
The Central India Horse

5th Indian Brigade
1st Bn, The Royal Fusiliers
3rd Bn, 1st Punjab Regiment
4th Bn (Outram's), 6th Rajputana Rifles
1st Field Regiment, Royal Artillery

11th Indian Infantry Brigade
2nd Bn, The Queen's Own Cameron Highlanders
1st Bn (Wellesley's), 6th Rajputana Rifles
4th Bn, 7th Rajput Regiment
4th Field Regiment, Royal Artillery

In September 1940 the Division received its third brigade from India:

7th Indian Infantry Brigade
1st Bn, The Royal Sussex Regiment
4th Bn, 11th Sikh Regiment
4th Bn, 16th Punjab Regiment
25th Field Regiment, Royal Artillery

By the time that 7 Brigade joined the Division it already had acquired its red eagle sign. Various stories circulated about the origins of the sign. The Divisional staff at the time dispelled all rumours, by providing the following detailed account. At the end of 1939, when Divisional Headquarters was located at Mena, the War Office ordered that the Divisional sign was to be a Red Eagle on a black background. The exchange of "minutes" then went something like this:

GSO 2 (Major Picken) to DDME (Major Windle): The Divisional sign is to be an eagle, side view, in red on black background. Size 8½ by 8½ inches. Please arrange, and let me know if there are any difficulties.

DDME to GSO 2: I can arrange this, and will have stencils made if design permits. Is there a sealed pattern of eagle, side view, or am I to design one?

GSO 2 to DDME: There is no sealed pattern. Have sent Warrant Officer, Army Education Corps to Giza Zoo to sketch eagle, side view. More details later.

GSO 2 to DDME: Herewith Warrant Officer's sketch of eagle, side view. I don't think much of it; but could it be stencilled?

(This note was accompanied by a sketch of a forlorn looking bird sitting on a perch. DDME discussed making stencils from it with the late Major Clarke, commanding one of the Workshop Sections. There were unfavourable comments).

DDME to GSO 2: Sketch returned herewith. Stencils can be made; but it looks more like a Dove of Peace, or love-sick Duck, than eagle. Suggest Mae West, side view. Could not be mistaken for any other Bird, and simple to make stencils.

GSO 2 to DDME: Cannot have Mae West since Eagle has been allotted by War Office. A better design being considered.

The Divisional Commander (General Scarlett) and the GSO 2 were now much concerned about producing a suitable design. Then one day General Scarlett walked into Henry Picken's office with a very good sketch of an eagle, side view, and said he had found the answer. Henry Picken thinks it had been copied from the label off a beer bottle, but General Scarlett always favoured his recollection that it was from an advertisement for Goodyear Tyres. About the same time, the DDME one day went into the Q Clerks Office and saw a very good rough sketch on a piece of blotting paper, which it is thought had been made by a temporary clerk, Private Page of 2 Camerons. This had been done in red and blue pencil, in heraldic style. The design was of an eagle about to take off with a rat clutched in its talons. The rat had the face of Hitler, and drops of blood were shown falling from it. DDME took this sketch to the GSO 2 who received it with thanks, but said that a somewhat similar design had already been approved by the Divisional Commander without the rat and drops of blood, since these were unauthorised.

DDME than adapted the GSO 2's design for stencilling on a square background. After GHQ approval had been obtained, this design was painted on all vehicles in the Division. Soon after this had been done, GHQ ordered that the square background should also have a white line, of about 2½ inches, at its base. This necessitated a new design, and had the effect of squashing the eagle up a bit; thus making it appear in full flight instead of taking off as originally shown. The eagle retained its outstretched wing form for about two years: and so far as we remember, sometime in 1941 the women of the Punjab at the instance of the Punjab's Prime Minister presented us with our first lot of shoulder flashes, to this design. However, both the design and the stencils had suffered from our many travels; and finally the master stencils were destroyed when the DDME's truck was burnt out.

General Tuker took over the Division in early 1942, and almost immediately expressed his strong disapproval of our very tattered looking eagle. He described it as "a Gull in Galoshes". He then re-designed the eagle on a square background, and in a form very similar to the original design – the necessity for the oblong background having by then been forgotten. In this re-designed form, the eagle survived the remainder of the War; and up to August 1947, when the Division came to its honourable end as part of the British Army.

*   *   *   *   *

First Steps with First Field

Within 24 hours of the outbreak of war, when we were convinced in 6th Medium Regiment in Muttra that we would be out of it for the duration, the telephone rang and the Colonel, who was a shade deaf, took the message that "Miles", the christian name of his Adjutant would leave for Nowshera next morning to join 1st Field Regiment to go overseas. As a young Assistant Adjutant I was ordered to take over and, as my first duty arrange a farewell party. Sometime after midnight a Chuprassi arrived on his bicycle to hand me the confirming telegram. Somewhat to my consternation it said "Wyld" not "Miles". The entire garrison accordingly moved to my bungalow with good suggestions as to what a young officer should take to war. It was fairly hilarious and suggestions were made and accepted including hog spears and a mashie niblick. In the middle of it all arrived, presumably by magic, my bearer Mohammed. A tearful goodbye was clearly called for but not at all. I was firmly told that if Sahib went to war then Mohammed goes to war too to look after him. What of his family? Allah would provide was the answer, which I found comforting. So a few hours later, escorted by the whole garrison, together with Mohammed and the hog spears the first Gunner Officer from Muttra set off for war.

On arrival at Nowshera we had about three days to find out what to take. The decision was to take guns, pick up horses in France but take saddlery. However, as we approached Suez we were told that we were to be mechanised. When we docked we were greeted with an imposing array of Morris Commercials and Austin Sevens. We looked nostalgically at our lovely saddlery and realised that not a single driver could drive anything except a horse. Officers took over the driving, we hitched up the guns with bits of rope and ferried them to Mena where, once we left the tarmac, our new "horses" could not cope and the rest of the war opened out as a vast digging operation.

In due course when more or less mobile we moved to Mersa Matruh. I well remember a Sunday morning breakfast when crumps were heard. Incredulous that the Sappers should be desecrating the Sabbath we all went outside. Up rushed Mohammed with his tin hat on pointing to six jolly-looking silver aeroplanes. We still could not believe it until sticks of bombs fell right through our Lines. Slit trenches were then actually dug and the visits of the Savoias were the regular order. Little damage was done because Mohammed had second sight and whenever he had his tin hat on one could safely give the alarm and, anyway the Italians for some extraordinary reason, as they like their food, were quite regular in choosing meal times to arrive.

Many will have vivid memories of the first Sidi Barrani battles. It was perhaps more difficult for Gunners than most, as we do have to range to hit the target but, in this instance, the long night approach march in complete silence precluded any preliminary ranging except to correct on to target. After the successful battles next morning and as night fell on the captured camp Nibeiwa, General Beresford-Peirse was "dining" in HQRA. He turned to me, as SCRA and said "John, do you realise that the success or failure of the whole attack on the last camp in the morning depends on you?" On being more explicit he was concerned that the guns would have enough ammunition. I hastily reassured him knowing that I had personally parked all the ammunition lorries in a secret hideout. However, with his remarks ringing in my ears, I hurried away, jumped into my truck and, ignoring wise warnings of uncleared mines all over the place, drove to my secret RV with the ammunition lorries. Not a sign of them except one whose driver told me that a senior officer had obligingly ordered them to scatter over a wide area. I had a happy night emulating the Pied Piper and we just made it to the guns in time.

After the Sidi Barrani battles, we were off by train from Alexandria to

Suez. It was New Year's Eve and we were very, very tired and dirty. As Staff Captain, I had to arrange accommodation on the RMS "Reina del Pacifico" which would be taking us to Eritrea. There she was in all her peacetime glory. On reaching my cabin at about 10 pm a genuine "Jeeves" arrived to ask me "What temperature do we like our bath – Sir?" After suitable reply I said that we were also very hungry and could something be done? The regular dinner hour was long since over, I was told, but that he would arrange with the Head Steward for a cold collation to be prepared. And what a cold collation it was, and our first introduction to the South African liqueur Van der Humm. Our blissful interlude of four days on this lovely ship (later to be sunk with great loss of life) was one of the most striking, and pleasant of all the war contrasts.

The first night that we spent in the jungle country of the Sudan we were not a little curious of the possibility of being visited by jungle animals. We huddled rather close together in our sleeping bags. Like good officers, we had of course washed before retiring and our chalumshis, still full of water, lay close to our heads. During the night we were all awoken by the patter of feet of a large animal and noisy lapping of water from the bowls by our heads. I think that we were all equally terrified. Then on, on a compass bearing across country to Kassala to be met by then Colonel Frank Messervy of Gazelle Force. The journey was an eyeopener as the natives on their donkeys, all armed with spear or sword, leapt off and fled screaming at the sight of their first motor vehicle.

Much could be written in more serious vein about the Eritrea campaign but nobody who was not there could believe that it could really happen in World War 2. My reminiscences are many and will have been shared by many. Perhaps some of the most striking are:

(a) Our bomber support. One Vickers Valencia, top speed 90 mph, "bombs" being hand grenades chucked out of the open door.

(b) Shortage of water. Only one source of supply so amicably shared by the British in the morning, the Italians in the afternoon, and the blue-bottomed baboons in the evening, and none would have dreamed of interfering with the other.

(c) The charge by 300 Eritrean cavalry, led by an Italian Major in white uniform and a cocked hat, against the guns. The Major was picked off by the Battery fitter with a newly acquired Boyes anti-tank rifle but quite a skirmish went on in the gun lines.

(d) The final assault on Keren by infantry carrying shields made of three layers of corrugated iron.

To these I would add two personal ones. After one of the attacks on Keren an Italian Gunner Brigadier was captured. He had been at an English public school and Oxford University, his mother was Scottish and his father Italian. He was delighted to be out of it all. He duly "dined" with HQRA that night and drew me aside and said words to the effect of "I have one great worry, I have a wife and two attractive daughters in Asmara, where you will soon be, and you know what soldiers are. Here is my visiting card and I would be so glad if you would go and call. They would be so pleased to have you to tea and perhaps you could look after them for me."

Food was actually pretty short in Eritrea and in the midst of the Keren battles a huge parcel arrived for me in the mail. This was a whole Stilton cheese in a Fortnum and Mason jar posted to me by an aunt on the second day of war. It not only caught up with me but, even in that temperature was in perfect condition.

*   *   *   *   *

On Joining

At the time of joining the Division I would not have considered myself a novice. I was serving when the war started. I had learnt the old Gunner skills on 6-inch Howitzers, and some hybrid ones on French 75s; I had welcomed the arrival of the 18/25 pounders and had put the old methods of "Link shooting" and the ponderous "Stages" of survey behind me as I trained myself and others in new methods of concentrating fire-power. In the field of tactical and combined training I had fairly extensive experience through the phases of preparing to fight the invader "on the beaches" and the, sometimes highly dangerous, eccentric and explosive ideas of those whose inventiveness would endeavour to replace weight of arms and manpower. From this defensive phase I had advanced with my regimental, brigade and divisional colleagues into the more mobile and aggressive formation training favoured by one General Montgomery – among others.

For all this I looked forward to becoming a subaltern in a 4th Indian Field Regiment rather warily. A Division which had fought with such distinction in the Eritrean, Western Desert and North African campaigns and emerged victorious and bedecked with honours would, understandably, have scant regard for such comparatively untried material. I was resolved to be "seen and not heard" until I had been able to prove myself worthy.

It was not like that. The confidence which abounded was not the intrinsically doubtful self-assurance which needs swagger and ostentation to support it. It was simply the quiet self-confidence emanating from the possession of knowledge, skills and character that had been subjected to numerous stringent trials and remained unshaken. There were no sensational tales of derring-do at which the newcomer must dutifully exclaim. Stories of the time of the Indian Mutiny could be encouraged from some of the old hands and how the "Timber Toppers" got their name, but nearer to the recent past it was possible only to revive jocular accounts of the "Ahwaz Bloodbath"; that apparently virtually bloodless decision to secure Iran's oilfields in which the Regiment had participated.

It soon became clear that one was being welcomed as a friend into a club of gentlemen of all ranks, race and creeds, and that the members of this club were quite confident that the new arrival would provide a response in every way worthy of them when the time came.

The rules of this club were committed to paper by an Indian Army officer:

"Your chief concern is not to endanger your comrade."

"Because of the risk that you may bring him, you do not light fires after sunset."

"You do not use his slit trench at any time."

"Neither do you park your vehicle near the hole in the ground in which he lives."

"You do not borrow from him, and particularly you do not borrow those precious fluids, water and petrol."

"You do not give him compass bearings which you have not tested and of which you are not sure."

"You do not leave any mess behind that will breed flies."

"You do not ask him to convey your messages, your gear, or yourself unless it is his job to do so."

"You do not drink deeply of any man's bottles, for they may not be replenished. You make sure that he has many before you take his cigarette."

"You do not ask information beyond your job, for idle talk kills men."

"You do not grouse unduly, except concerning the folly of your own commanders. This is allowable. You criticise no other man's commanders."

"Of those things which you do do, the first is to be hospitable and the second is to be courteous. The day is long in the desert and there is time to be helpful to those who share your adventure. A cup of tea, therefore, is proffered to all comers – it is your handshake and your badge of association. Over the tea mugs the good mannered guest transacts his business expeditiously, gossips shop for a little, and gets him gone."

"This code is the sum of fellowship in the desert. It knows no rank nor any exception."

The little incident that symbolised for me the way in which 4th Indian Division was magnificent in everyday things was my first sight of one of the Battery cable-laying trucks. It happened on my first day in the Regiment. I had come from an environment of relatively modern, certainly new, equipment; if one could demonstrate superiority over other formations it was mostly in appearances; in comprehensiveness of equipment, camouflage, march discipline, and turnout, as well as in the way in which one carried out the numerous technical and tactical drills (and, for most, they were still drills which had to be remembered!).

There was this truck which seemed to materialise out of the sand. It had no superstructure. It bore an astonishing resemblance to one of those toy cars made of boxes and pram wheels which used to delight aspiring young racing drivers. There were two Gunners in what remained of the front seats and entirely exposed to the elements except where the bonnet protected them. There were two men sitting above the rear sheels in what remained of the load carrying rear. The cable-laying equipment and a bracket for an LMG looked gaunt and bare. Everything was sand-coloured including the men, so that it could well have been a sculpture.

I think that this was the only occasion that the deep pride in the Regiment came to the surface:

"That's the finest 'Monkey-truck' in the Division!
They have always kept going and always got through"

– then a rather embarrassed laugh. I have always remembered that small boast; partly because of its rarity, but mostly because I think it contains the secret of the old hands in 4th Indian: a simple pride in carrying out whatever task was theirs supremely well; whatever the conditions, whateve the odds. At all levels they were, in their way, craftsmen.

SIDI BARRANI

In the Spring of 1940, 5th Indian Infantry Brigade was deployed in scattered encampments along 150 miles of coast between Alexandria and Mersa Matruh, 7th Indian Infantry Brigade (less 4/7 Rajputs) and Divisional HQ were encamped at Mena as GHQ Middle East Reserve. In September the Italian Army invaded Egypt from Libya with two regular Italian divisions, two colonial divisions and one Blackshirt division. They took Sidi Barrani, about 250 miles from Alexandria. By December the Division (with 16 British Brigade under command to provide the third brigade pending the arrival of 7th Indian Infantry Brigade) was poised to attempt to throw back the Italians from Egypt.

*   *   *   *   *

Babu at Sidi Barrani

When war started in 1939 I was in India. My personal servant was a Madrassi nicknamed Babu; well-trained, quick-witted and emancipated; a paragon.

In 1940 I was sent to Egypt to command a Brigade (11th) in the 4th Indian Division and Babu came with me. I could not dissuade him – "Master" was going to war and he would go with Master! I pointed out that he would not be on the strength, that he would not get any rations: he would probably starve and in any case he would not be allowed to embark at Bombay: if he managed this, he would not be allowed to disembark in Egypt! I wasted my breath, he did not stowaway, but just insinuated himself! He made himself indispensable, too useful to be sent off the ship. His disembarkation at Port Said was carried out with an air such that his Brigadier "Master" began to wonder which of the two was the VIP.

He soon adapted himself to active service. His civilian clothing almost imperceptibly became military until he was indistinguishable from a soldier, though at times he would appear in a pork-pie hat and a long coat with brass buttons for special occasions. Where he kept his changes of gear was a mystery: however the Brigadier's bedding-roll was not always as small as perhaps it should have been and the cushions of his car often

10

had knobbly lumps under them. He made friends of course with the Mess staff to whom at length he gave orders, and had contacts with others of importance such as Quartermaster Sergeants!

He drove a car and took turns with the regular driver. He delighted in driving with a flag on the bonnet and his joy knew no bounds when one day he found himself chauffeur to the Divisional Commander, red flag and all! He made no secret of his ambition to drive a Commander-in-Chief or even a Viceroy, an ambition he achieved though this belongs to another story. In short, blind eyes and deaf ears were turned and Babu, who had no right whatsoever to be there, became accepted as a cheerful, useful and picturesque member of the Brigade HQ.

But there was a limit, clearly explained and equally clearly understood. Although he had come thus far and made himself so useful, he was to have no place in any fighting. When the Brigade was to go into action Babu was to stay with the transport. So on 5th December 1940 with the 4th Indian Division advanced prior to attacking at Sidi Barrani, Babu said farewell to his master and stayed with the transport. Somewhat tearfully he pinned a little Catholic medallion of St Anthony in the lining of the Brigadier's tin-hat and with obvious regret stayed behind. In parenthesis, Babu was a Hindu but nothing if not broad-minded.

The battle for Sidi Barrani needs no description here. It is enough to say that it lasted three days, was a success and for the most part took place in a severe sandstorm. During the last day with the sandstorm at its height and the battle at its climax, a voice was heard crying in the desert "Where is my Master – where is my Master?" There was no mistaking it. Out of the storm appeared Babu, his face white with dust and his hands deep in the bulging pockets of an Italian General's greatcoat! He was grinning from ear to ear. What was he doing here – where had he been? His reception was by no means kindly. Did he not realise that by dressing up in Italian uniform he was in danger of being shot or at least of being sent to a prisoner-of-war cage? He would have to stay with us now, so the sooner he could make himself useful the better. There was not much he could do anyway except open some bully-beef and brew up some tea. But Babu knew better.

Had he now been roaming the battlefield and had he not been thinking always of his master? True, he had disobeyed orders but, "What would Master say to this?" Hands dived deep into protruding pockets and out slid slabs of chocolate, tins of macaroni, bottles of sauce and even a dead hen "specially for Master"!

After our alfresco repast, moderately cooked and thankfully eaten, Babu was again taken to task for exposing himself to danger in defiance of orders, whereupon he quietly produced from yet another pocket two automatic pistols of Italian origin, loaded and cocked – for self-defence – and a bundle of thousand-lira notes – just in case!

Truly my Paragon was also a Paladin.

*   *   *   *   *

With 3rd/1st Punjab Regiment at Sidi Barrani

One of my Viceroy Commissioned Officers was badly wounded in the head at our first battle at Sidi Barrani. He survived evacuation to a Cairo hospital where I visited him some weeks later.

Due to the operation on his head he was paralysed down one side, but he showed me with pride that he was beginning to get movement back. With his left hand he picked up his right and said "Look Sahib, I can move," as he slowly managed to move one finger of the paralysed hand.

I did not see him again until six years later when I rejoined by Battalion: by that time it was a parachute battalion and he was the Subedar Major.

At the cost of under 700 casualties, 4th Indian Division destroyed four Italian Divisions and took more than 20,000 prisoners at Sidi Barrani. Then while others pursued, the Division was withdrawn and sent to the Sudan at Christmas time in 1940. The new task for the Division, along with 5th Indian Division, was to drive the Italians out of Eritrea.

7 and 11 Brigades reached Sudan by sea and 5 Brigade came overland following the Nile. By the third week of January 1941 7 Brigade was directed on the Eritrean coast road towards Massawa, the only Red Sea port in Eritrea; 11 Brigade was on the route towards Kassala in the centre, and 5 Brigade was approaching Kassala on the right flank from Atbara on the Nile to the North West.

The Commander of 7 Brigade, Brigadier Briggs, was given the task in February 1941 of advancing south along the coast to relieve the pressure being extended by the Italians on Keren and to seize a sea entry and base: to accomplish this 7 Brigade was reinforced and became Briggs Force.

THE EAGLE RANGES WIDELY
Supplies and Transport – Eritrean Style

4/16 Punjabis were at the small haven of Mersa Taclai by the second week of February 1941, about 100 miles north of Massawa, and the fortress of Keren about 50 miles to its west. Supply through Mersa Taclai provided some unusual aspects. The 7 Brigade Staff Captain (Captain Hughes of the 2/11 Royal Sikhs) wrote:

"The problem was a curious one as we had to cater for food for British, French, Indians, West Africans and Sudanese. Native dhows had to be used and as there was no standard tonnage our loading was not planned on Staff College lines. Escorts were provided by Punjab Mussulmans of 4/16 Punjabis. Some dhows were never seen again and presumably were lost at sea, others arrived with the escort so seasick that they had to be carried ashore."

*   *   *   *   *

Some further light has been shed by the 4/16th themselves.

*   *   *   *   *

In these early days of the war, there were no sophisticated beach landing units or equipment and the mixed force of British, Indian, French and African troops had to be supplied on an *ad hoc* basis. Native dhows with PM escorts from the Battalion had to be used. The Battalion QM Captain Tony Henley was put in charge of the "Base" at Mersa Taclai on the Eritrean coast and when the Battalion passed through it he recalls that they were dossed down in an insect infested piece of scrub. When the time came for supper the CO said, "Well, I suppose we had better call for the bully beef and biscuits" – which he did. The Khansama duly appeared carrying a concoction served in the traditional way in a chilunchee. "What's that?" asked Colonel Sidney Lavender, the CO. "Sandgrouse and Bustard Pie, sahib," came the answer. This was the result of the Sapper's early morning shift at the well he was developing a few miles from the base, supplemented by a chance successful shot at a bustard on the way home. The pie was topped with desiccated potatoes, kindly provided from the Foreign Legion Battalion's rations. It was a great improvement on bully beef and biscuits.

As the base at Mersa Taclai developed, a few adventurous local Arabs appeared from nowhere. A useful addition to the garrison was the AA gunnery officer. He was a war-time recruitment from the Sudan administrative service in which he was quite senior and spoke several Sudani dialects. One morning, some local Arabs appeared with some highly coloured fish which they were offering for sale. After considerable bargaining the gunner reached a very good contract with these Arabs. They were to produce each day by 6 am sufficient fish for five officers. The cost of this extra messing was ½ piastre per day.

Later, the original sailor, a great character known as Tar Paulin who dealt with the ship to shore movement of men and supplies, was replaced by a young regular naval officer whose experience appeared to be limited to text books. After the usual preliminaries and having taken over from the original incombent, he said " and what arrangements have been made for my accommodation?" The reply was: "Well, you see all those sand dunes down by the shore, some of them are already occupied, but you can help yourself to any unoccupied one which you fancy!"

*　　*　　*　　*　　*

Before joining in the infantry battalions' race to Massawa, which the 4/16 Punjab Regiment won with its carriers, in the first week of April 1941 that Battalion was investing the Enghiart position; an operation in which Briggs Force tied down some eight enemy colonial battalions and supporting artillery while a direct assault was being made on the fortress of Keren about 10 miles to the south west.

The Battalion was operating 11 miles or so up a dry nullah leading to Mount Enghiart. Water was rationed to one pint a day a head as it had to be transported by camels for the whole Force (about 600 camels had had to be collected for the cross country move to the area from the coast).

One day B Company, 4/16th, having had an arduous day in intense heat had finished their water ration early and were suffering from extreme thirst. The young Company Commander asked for an extra supply. After a severe lecture on water discipline from the CO his request was granted. Unfortunately though, the Company Commander had not consulted Subedar Daim Kham – whose service exceeded his own by 30 years.

When the Subedar discovered what had happened he also upbraided his Company Commander, and when the extra water arrived he formed up the Company and publicly poured all the precious water into the sand. B Company's "izzat" was restored; even though at the expense of terrible thirst.

Two years later, when this much loved and feared VCO was a prisoner of war in Germany, the Battalion was relaxing and training in Cyprus. The Company Commander had occasion to believe that the men were failing to produce anything like the zeal and speed of which they were capable: his reaction – "You would not be so slow about it if Subedar Daim Kham was here." It was enough for them to redouble their efforts. The Subedar's personality had reached out over the barbed wire and over borders and seas.

On 27th March 1941 the Central India Horse entered Keren and the subsequent pursuit to Asmara was followed by the Italian surrender there on 1st April. Briggs Force, of 5 Brigade and their friends, took the surrender of 550 officers and 10,000 troops at Massawa on 8th April. In 66 days 4th and 5th Indian Divisions and 1st South African Division had captured Eritrea, expelled the Italians from Abyssinia and safeguarded Sudan.

4th Indian Division returned to Egypt; to find a very changed situation. Six Italian and three German divisions had been ferried into North Africa, the latter comprising Rommel's Afrika Korps. Tobruk, with a mixed British and Australian garrison was being besieged by two thirds of the enemy's total force. Syria was in grave danger of being handed over by "Vichy" French sympathisers to the Germans.

General Wavell was faced with a familiar task of making many bricks with very little straw. He sent two brigades of 7th Australian Division and 5th Indian Brigade with six Free French battalions to Syria in May. In June he mounted operation BATTLEAXE *in Cyrenaica with the aim of raising the siege of Tobruk and drawing the enemy back to Derna. For this battle, HQ 4th Indian Division had 11th Indian Brigade and 22nd Guards Brigade, and the armoured element was represented by 4th Armoured Brigade with the slow and heavy "I" tanks and 7th Armoured Brigade with the lighter and faster cruiser tanks.*

Although 11 Brigade almost succeeded in capturing its objective, Halfaya Pass, operation BATTLEAXE *had to be called off in the face of German tank superiority and the novel and devastating use of the German 88 mm AA gun in the anti-tank role.*

British losses were 1,000 killed and wounded and 96 tanks lost. However, 50 of the superior German tanks had been destroyed and a strong enemy attack on Tobruk had certainly been considerably postponed.

5 Brigade experienced bitter fighting in Syria and took very heavy casualties: 1 Royal Fusiliers in particular were decimated. As always, though there was a lighter side.

When 5th Indian Brigade moved into Syria with the Free French Forces one of the captures made on the way to Damascus was a very smart civilian Chevrolet saloon car which was being used by the Vichy French.

It was not long before the Free French Command learnt of this and a deputation arrived at 5 Brigade Headquarters to claim the prize.

The Brigade Major managed to persuade the Free French representative that this was just an unfounded rumour. This was no mean feat because it was done while leaning against the car, which had already been subjected to rapid surgery and face-lift in that its mudguards had been cut back to accommodate desert tyres and it was still wet from its new coat of desert camouflage paint.

The same car was used for many years for selected officers to motor to Cairo on leave from the desert. During this time it survived an unexploded shell ripping through it from one side to the other (taking the dashboard with it); also coming unscathed through many Military Police check points by reason of its excellent documentation and the military number on its bonnet, which more properly belonged to a more official Chevrolet.

*   *   *   *   *

Part of the Fight on the Escarpment – Operation BATTLEAXE

"Coast Force" moved up from its forming-up area in the early hours of the morning. The Mahrattas led, with the "Raj Rif" following, while the 25th Field Regiment were ready to give support. The units sought the cover of the hills several miles east of Halfaya, and worked their way along the glacis. This was done for fear of a tank attack from the defences which ran across the plain to the sea from the foot of the pass. The Indians climbed slowly across the ridges and gullies making for the head of the road. Six "I" tanks accompanied the right company to deal with any strong points met on the plain.

As the infantry went forward from their start line in the morning light, heavy fire was opened from the ridges and from the top of the escarpment, where observation was good. Casualties were suffered but the Indian infantry pushed on with the utmost determination working their way along the ravines and up the slopes. Individual Tommy-gunners climbed the rocky wadis to fight to the death with the enemy outposts. Sepoy Babu Desai of the Mahrattas, only 18 years old, took command of his section when its commander was wounded. When the company was held up, he picked up his Bren gun, rushed across the open under heavy fire, and brought the gun into action from the flank, enabling the company to move on again. Then he was wounded in the leg and his platoon commander told him to go back to the Regimental Aid Post to have the wound dressed. But Babu Desai had other views. He rushed the gun that had wounded him, killing the gunner and making the others run. Then his leg gave way under him, but still he had to be forcibly placed on a stretcher before he would even consider his own troubles.

While 5 Brigade (which had recouped the losses resulting from the Syrian campaign and had been rejoined by those who had been taken prisoner) was still in northern Syria trying to keep order among squabbling tribes, 7 Brigade from the "Box" at Baqqush was despatched to relieve Australian troops in the Siwa and Giarabub oases. From there, with Central India Horse and supporting arms, the Brigade carried out long range patrolling, harassing the enemy.

By September 1941 the dispersal of troops all over the Middle East could end. Syria, Iran and Iraq had been secured against the Axis powers. The losses in Greece and Crete had been made good. New equipment was flowing into Egypt and the 8th Army, comprising 13 and 30 Corps, came into being.

4th Indian Division, having recovered its three Brigades: 5th, 7th and 11th, took up position on the Libyan border about 40 miles south east of Salum. With 2nd New Zealand Division, with whom 4th Indian was to have many memorable close associations, and with 1st Army Tank Brigade, 4th Indian was to become part of 13 Corps for the "Crusader" operation; designed to bring the enemy armour into battle with 30 Corps (7th Armoured Division, 1 South African Division and 22 Guards Brigade) and to relieve Tobruk.

4th Indian ran into heavy resistance from the fortified encampments round Libyan Omar and Omar Nuovo 15 miles south of Capuzzo.

Two of the Division's Field Regiments produce stories of the battle for the Omars; covering both the heat of action and the inevitable muddle of war.

*   *   *   *   *

The Battle for the Omars

With the enemy swarming in the area, a clash was not long delayed. The Panzer columns, having crossed the frontier wire south of the Omars, turned into the north in a wide sweep, intent on destruction. Supply columns were shot up and dispersed, the vehicles fleeing in all directions. At 1700 hours on 25th November 4/11 Sikhs and 1 Field Regiment, having completed their escort duties, had returned to their masking positions to the south-east of Cova. An armoured car raced up and reported an enemy tank force to be approaching. One troop of 11 Battery accompanied the Sikhs into the Omars; the remainder of 1 Field Regiment prepared for action.

At 0730 hours 25 tanks appeared in the south, fired a few ranging rounds and withdrew. 1 Field Regiment deployed its batteries in echelon, dug slit trenches and waited. At 0840 the Panzers reappeared on the horizon and slowly crept forward. Twenty-eight heavy Mark III and Mark IV types advanced in fleet formation in lines five abreast, with 30 yards interval between tanks and 70 yards between ranks. The much debated clash of tank versus field gun was imminent.

At 2,000 yards the Panzers opened fire, halting to lay their cannon and maintaining long-range machine-gun fire while in movement. They closed from the south-east and concentrated on 52 Battery on the left of 1 Field Regiment's position. The gunners, lying beside their pieces and waiting for the word, suffered heavily. The tanks crept closer and closer; one gun after another was struck. Still the dour artillerymen waited. When the Panzers were only 800 yards away and the final rush imminent, the gunners sprang into action. The sharp bark of the 25 pounders cut against the crack of the 75 mm cannon as tanks and field guns belaboured each other. For 10 minutes, in close deadly encounter, the adversaries swapped punches. The tanks flinched first, broke away and lumbered to the west for 400 yards, where a low dune afforded hull-down protection. Ten tanks in line, the battle continued. When the artillery fire grew unbearable the

Panzers charged 52 Battery head on. Among the strewn bodies of their comrades, the gunners, working like mad, kept the enemy armour at a distance. At 300 yards the Panzer line broke and scrambled away to the south-east, with the vengeful guns buffeting them. Seven smashed tanks dotted the plain, and troops of South African anti-tank gunners, which had arrived too late to join the action, finished off another as it hobbled away.

(Water-Carrier Rattan Singh of the Sikhs, whose imperturbability on the slopes of Samana in Eritrea had earned him mention, was preparing breakfast for his comrades in a slit trench when the tanks appeared. The guns and Panzers fought it out over his head. The battle over, he emerged to announce that tea was ready.)

This magnificent stand in the open and without support, cost 1 Field Regiment 18 killed and 42 wounded. 52 Battery sustained 42 casualties out of 73 of all ranks in action. The discipline and courage of the artillery-men had halted the Panzer foray before it could reach the supply routes to the north of the Omars. This trouncing, however, failed to satisfy the enemy, and during that afternoon another 28 tanks crawled upon the southern perimeter of Omar Nuova. The purpose of this approach remains a mystery, as the enemy must have known that he was advancing against his own minefields. At 4,000 yards the tanks opened fire. Receiving no response, they continued to close. The drama of the encounter drew the infantry from their slit trenches; every vehicle became a miniature grand-stand. For a mile the Panzers crept up, firing, halting, studying their targets, firing anew and steadily closing in. The gunners of 1 Field Regi-ment crouched and bided their time until the first tanks topped a low contour 1,000 yards away. Then the artillery commander sprang to his feet with a shout and a salvo from the 25-pounders crashed home. Furiously plying shell, the gunners blew the leading tanks to pieces. The Panzers tacked to the west under punishment, circling the perimeter and providing a target for every gun in Omar Nuovo. Even 7 Medium Regi-ment depressed muzzles and pumped heavy shell at the German armour. Five tanks reeled to a stop and six more were disabled as they fled. Many others carried heavy damage out of range.

Notes from 25th Field Regiment, RA

By now we had about surrounded the Omars and the Regiment moved to a position to the west of them to support the initial attack. The first day of the battle ended with a part of Libyan Omar still in enemy hands. The Italians had profited from the tuition of their German masters, and instead of stone sangars – an easy target to observe, they had dug well sited strong points from which all spoil had been removed and thus were quite invisible until one was on top of them. Each post, though independent of each other was inter-supporting and it was virtually impossible to direct observed fire on them with any accuracy. Casualties were very heavy among the assaulting troops, particularly the 4/16 Punjab and Royal Sussex with whom we were involved. Every enemy post was packed with light machine guns and anti-tank guns.

A day or two later the guns were moved to a position north of the Omars, but whenever we opened fire we were shelled from the rear or so it seemed – later it dawned on us that this opposition was coming from the Capuzzo area, still in enemy hands. It was very uncomfortable, but fortunately little harm was done. It took us sometime to appreciate what ground was ours and what was not. The enemy were equally in the dark and I can still remember missing a German officer and staff car who drove innocently across the front of my OP in what he obviously considered friendly country!

The battle now took a bizarre turn, for unknown to us, a Panzer group, later rumoured to have been led by Rommel himself, was working round our rear and units of it began to appear in the most unexpected places. A New Zealand officer came into our area and told us that strange-looking tanks marked with black crosses had passed the head of his supply column, but were so intent on their own business that they had failed to take any notice of him. Then our ammunition lorries failed to arrive, and because of this it was decided that I should take the gun towers and eight limbers to the Brigade "B" Echelon area for ammunition – in the light of hindsight a somewhat foolhardy move, but we must have been desperately short.

When I started the scene was peaceful enough. A long line of prisoners coming out of the Omars and the war seemed good. It was late afternoon. However the moment I arrived in the supply area I was aware of a change in the atmosphere and I sensed all was not well. The troops around were in a state of unease – too many wearing tin hats and many standing on their vehicles staring at the horizon or the sky. As I approached the ammunition point three hostile planes came over and did some strafing, and to the westward a mass of vehicles of all description were moving towards us. On enquiry I was told there were enemy tanks in the vicinity, but I was inclined to discount this. The officer commanding the ammunition point thought differently and had loaded up and was ready to move.

The mass of vehicles we had seen (mentioned above) were certainly ours and started to move through us, but then about a mile away I saw another column that I could not at first identify, though their appearance awoke vague memories. Suddenly I identified them as the exact replica of a Panzer unit, a picture of which I had seen in the *Sphere* and *Illustrated London News*, a copy of which someone had left in our mess. The unit was led by three or four eight-wheeled armoured cars and a section of guns drawn by troop-carrying tractors. The armoured cars fired occasionally, but seemed content to keep their distance and move alongside our own column. I was bewildered, so flagged down one of our own vehicles, which obligingly stopped, and inquired of the occupant (a Major) if he could tell me what was happening and where they were going. The reply was that he had no idea, but was following his Brigadier and he believed the opposition had broken through and was behind them. I pointed out the Panzer unit, virtually alongside although some way off, and our reaction was to burst out laughing. He then continued his journey, but the ammunition point commander who had joined us decided that this was no place for his organisation and without further thought shot off with the ammunition lorries. I was left alone with my gun tractors and empty limbers.

Dusk was now approaching and where I was was no place to stay. So I made my way to our Brigade "B" Echelon area in the hope that they had not been carried away with the tide. They had not, but had experienced some strafing from the air and had casualties. The Echelon commander was without orders and communication with Brigade HQ had broken down. I told him what had happened to me, and in the circumstances he concentrated all our units in case orders were received during the night to move. At some stage Tony English (Battery Captain of 31/58 Battery) appeared, who had been on the same mission as myself.

Eventually a laager was formed, all weapons were dug out – some rifles, two bren guns and an anti-tank rifle were assembled and distributed. Men were set to dig holes round the perimeter. It was thus hoped that by bluff we might scare off any would-be hostile approach during the night.

Verey lights now began to shoot skywards all round us, though I think few appreciated the significance of this. I found some rum in our officers' mess truck and soon we were feeling in much better form. A constant stream of visitors began to arrive, all inquiring whereabouts of their units.

A senior officer of a Tank Regiment was told that there was no need for alarm as we had formed an impregnable position. One laughs at these incidents now and one cannot help wondering why everyone manning the laager showed such a lack of concern. Perhaps it was the rum!

All night we heard the rumble of vehicles moving round us, and some were certainly tracked, which must have been German tanks rallying – hence the Verey lights. Sometime after these defensive measures had been taken Tony English remembered that our Quartermaster had some armour-piercing rifle ammunition and asked him if he had issued it. The answer was in the negative, the explanation being that it had taken him (the Quarter-master) a very long time to get hold of and he would probably never be able to get any more – quite an argument ensued over this point of view!

At daybreak Tony and I decided that we must return to the ammunition point, in case there was still some ammunition on the ground. An air of unreality was everywhere, numerous parties with no officers passed us, quite ignorant of what they were about or where they were going. We found two Jiwans still guarding an area which had been a dump of some sort, but from which everything had been removed – we took them up in our trucks. Further on we saw some deserted trucks and on approaching with a view to appropriating them, found they had been looted, but were in running order – we did the obvious thing. Next we saw some movement of men on a slight rise, we approached very cautiously and found some dejected Indian orderlies who belonged to a dressing station. They warned us to be off as they were prisoners. However as there were no guards we persuaded them to come along with us. Nevertheless this brought home to us that the enemy must be very close so we returned to the Brigade "B" Echelon area of the night before to find that they had received orders to move at once to the Omars and join their respective units.

Tony and I decided to have one more try at finding the ammunition point area and at last we found it. As anticipated there was plenty of ammunition still on the ground. We had partly loaded up when about 20 obviously hostile tanks appeared. Luckily they were otherwise occupied and may not have seen us. Anyhow we beat it.

We were not sorry to be back in the Omars, although it was still partly occupied by the enemy. During the morning German tanks attacked our positions, but the brunt of this was taken by, I think, 1st Field Regiment RA. In conclusion I may say that during my absence our ammunition lorries had turned up, so my exercise had been fruitless and of unnecessary risk to all concerned – especially the guns which had been immobilised by the lack of their towers.

Attack by 4/16th Punjabis

This was perhaps the Battalion's toughest battle.

Sidi Omar was an island fortress in the desert, west of Solum.

The Royal Sussex penetrated the position sustaining very heavy casualties – then we passed through them to complete the operation. The invincible (or so it was thought) "I" Tanks (Matildas) went forward and were all knocked out by the deadly German 88 mm. Colonel Lavender then launched three companies into the fray (A, C and D). They battled forward bravely taking one line of trenches after another but suffered so many casualties that at last they stopped. By now the strength of these three companies was reduced and only one officer was left, Captain Herbert. Lieut McGarity was killed.

Two nights later orders were received for another attack to be launched to complete the job and the CO went forward that night to give the orders for the attack. I went with him as IO.

We found "Bertie" Herbert in a subterranean cemented Italian dugout, well stocked with wines and furniture. Elsewhere dead Italians lay everywhere and we had to walk on them along the trenches.

"Bertie" was glad to see us and entertained us with wine but as he heard the CO's orders he became very silent. When asked if he had any questions he thought for a minute then asked the following questions, knowing full well the answers.

Q. What is the estimated strength of the enemy?

A. About 500 men.

Q. What is the total strength of the three attacking coys?

A. 110 men.

Q. What is the frontage of the attack?

A. 800 yards.

Soon afterwards the CO and I left and I had the feeling we would not see "Bertie" again.

The attack went in a few hours later but was only partially successful. Captain Herbert was reported missing and some time later when the position was finally forced to surrender his body was found, all by itself well to the front.

The November CRUSADER *operation developed into the initial heavy and confused battles with enemy armour in the Djebel Achdar, and the subsequent pursuit of the Axis forces to Benghazi. In the period from the fighting from the Omars and Christmas Day in Benghazi the Division had taken 6,000 prisoners and had destroyed 51 tanks and 27 aircraft.*

Losses in the Division had been 178 officers and 2,455 other ranks. The Division at the end of pursuit was dispersed over 150 miles of desert with 11 Brigade, less 1/6 Rajputana Rifles garrisoning Tobruk, 5 Brigade between Giovanni Berta and Barce, and 7 Brigade about to move from Derna to Benghazi. However, Rommel was about to receive massive reinforcement and to demonstrate his ability for quick and effective reaction which had not yet been understood by all his opponents. By the third week in January a formidable force was advancing on Benghazi from the south, and the confusion of the withdrawal from the Djebel Achdar began.

*   *   *   *   *

The 4/16th Punjabis and a Bedouin Souvenir

My memories of this event are rather muddled and not too accurate – I was acting as Liaison Officer at 7 Brigade HQ. When Rommel struck back from Agedabia and cut off the Brigade Group in Benghazi.

We, Brigade HQ and the 4/16th, started to evacuate the town, travelling north with C Company leading, the Battalion HQ and the other companies. Before going very far the column halted and we heard that the Germans had cut us off. It was pourng with rain. It was decided that C Company should hold the Germany during the rest of the night.

The rest of the Brigade HQ and A, B and D Companies somehow managed to turn round and headed southwards hoping to cut across the enemy's line of communication unnoticed.

At this stage I was sent for and instructed to guide the column as navigation officer. I managed to get my bearings and we left the road shortly afterwards. There was a tense moment when we had to go through a gap in a minefield and no one could remember whether the Royal Engineers had closed the gap or not. Sandbags were piled on to the floor of a truck and we drove through and with a sigh of relief we reached the other end without being blown up.

After passing through the minefield the column was halted: still in the pitch dark and rain. Owing to the fact that we had a long run in front of us to (we hoped) Tobruk, and there would be no further petrol made available – the Brigade Commander (Brigadier Briggs) gave the order for every vehicle which was not absolutely essential to be destroyed and the petrol drained from the tanks and stored. I smashed up my little captured Italian Fiat car and settled down with a compass on the roof of a 15 cwt truck. When all was ready the order was given to set off. This we did, Brigade

HQ, A, B, D Companies together with a battery of Field Artillery and Royal Engineers; some 100 vehicles, I suppose. I navigated the column southwards through the night and just before dawn turned south-east and then east. Shortly after dawn we crossed Rommel's axis south of Msus. Here, some tanks approached, but thinking we were stronger than we actually were, refrained from attacking. However when most of the column had passed them they rushed in and cut off the tail of the column which consisted of Dogra elements of the Battalion. On we travelled, expecting every moment to be bombed but our fears were never realised – presumably the Luftwaffe was too busy elsewhere – certainly the other columns of the Brigade who had broken out separately were bombed heavily.

I cannot remember how long I sat on top of the truck navigating without any sleep, but it seemed to be days until at last we saw some vehicles, armoured cars, making for us – not knowing whether they were friendly or not we stopped, and then found out to our relief that they were South Africans.

They escorted us back to Tobruk where we waited to hear how other elements of the Brigade Group had fared. Rommel's advance continued and we fell back to an area near Sidi Barrani and commenced digging fortifications. While there, we were surprised to see, one day, two of our officers who had been left behind at Benghazi come into the camp, Captains McKinley and Easton; later Captain Chase (MTO) also came back. They had very interesting stories to tell. On that night at Benghazi when capture seemed inevitable, these three slipped away before dawn and made off into the desert. There they met some Bedouins who helped them, and after walking probably over 1,000 miles they passed through the German positions again and rejoined the 8th Army. Some of the Jawans also got away and one, a clerk, lived with Bedouins for a long time – until we recaptured Benghazi again a year or so later, I think. When the Battalion passed through Benghazi on its way to the Tunisian battlefields, the headman of these Bedouins presented the Battalion with a goat, which became the Regimental mascot, or rather, the Officer's Mess mascot. This goat, named "Rastus", henceforward travelled widely with the Battalion to Tunis, Cairo, Jerusalem, Tripoli (Syria) and eventually back to India. It was notorious for its odour and I was its principal benefactor. After I left the Battalion at Peshawar for the Staff College, I heard that Rastus had finally proved too much of a burden on the Battalion and had been "put away".

11 Brigade's Rearguard at El Faida

Sergeant Grey, DCM MM of the 2nd Camerons tells of the afternoon of 1st February when a force of lorried infantry with a recce tank and some armoured cars approached his platoon in its hurriedly prepared holding position.

"About 1530 hours they arrived. An armoured car and a tank, followed by lorries came streaming over the top. Twenty Kittyhawks paid no attention and cruised above us as if on Bank Holiday. The lorries stopped on the top and the tank and armoured cars came on, watched breathlessly by everyone, until they got neatly picked off by an anti-tank gun as they came round the last corner – nicely within Bren range. The crews only ran a yard or two!

"Then the party started. The Germans deployed well out of range, got their mortars, machine-guns and a battery going, and rushed stuff over and into our hill without stopping. Meanwhile one could see the infantry dodging about in the bushes on the hillside. Things looked ugly, as presumably we were on a last-man-last-round racket, and it was going to be a night party. No wire and five hundred yards to each platoon front!

"But as dusk fell word came to thin out at 1915 hours and leave by 1930 hours – a big relief as there seemed to be a lot of Germans. By 1930 hours it was dark and I went out to bring in one of the forward sections.

"I went off down the hill and saw some people coming my way. So I shouted 'Is that McKay's section?' 'Yes!' came the answer. So I went on to tell them to sit on top of the hill. When I came nearer I felt that something was wrong. Something was! A large German jumped out from behind a bush and pinned me before I could think. Then a German and an Italian officer came running up, took my rifle and equipment off me, stuck automatics in my stomach and back, while the Italian speaking perfect English, said 'Lead us to your comrades; tell them to surrender and you will be well treated.' I feigned sickness and stupidity and asked for water, but got kicked in the stomach by the German. There seemed no alternative, so I pointed to my left and the German ordered his platoon to go off in that direction, presumably to do a flanking movement. I started off up the hill, with the officers on either side, and stumbling in the dark managed to bring my platoon well onto my flank.

Then I aimed for their position, which I could just distinguish in the dark. I heard a Jock say 'Here the b––– s come.' Then the Italian said 'Shout to them to surrender!' So I shouted 'McGeogh, McGeogh!' (I knew he was a good shot), got within ten yards of them, shouted 'Shoot' and fell flat. The boys shot and got the German in the head and the Italian in the stomach. Grand! So off I ran and rejoined the platoon. By then we were long past our withdrawal time; so back we went, and after a bit of bayonet work by the rear platoon, jumped into lorries and drove off with the Germans lining the road behind us, popping at us at point-blank range.

"When we left Faida we reckoned that by tea-time to-morrow we would be busy again."

* * * * *

"Q" – Lest We Forget

A withdrawal in desert, often almost impassable, terrain where enemy columns may come from so many directions and where great distances are involved, is a big test of morale and skill for everyone but a special strain is put on "Q": that 4th Indian Division was able to carry out the withdrawal from Benghazi with a loss of only about 600 men out of a strength of about 12,000, was due to a significant extent to the splendid support provided by the "Q" Services. The problems of the withdrawal were graphically described in *The Tiger Kills*.

"In retirements in which units are hopelessly mixed up and scattered over wide distances, it is the supply columns which carry the greatest strain. A dozen times each day 'Q' services find themselves with almost insuperable problems. Units come out of nowhere, to be placed under command, to be fed and watered. There is never enough transport to supply all; the shuttling of vehicles takes on the intricacy of a jig-saw puzzle. Supply dumps are constantly shifting. Officers go on recon-naissance in search of them and never come back. Units struck off ration strength as captured walk in next day demanding supplies. Above everything else looms the liquid problem. There are never enough water tins to go round, and never petrol tins which do not leak. (After this war some sardonic essayist will find a fruitful subject in the British Army's determination to capture enough 'Jerry cans' to serve, rather than to manufacture non-leakable water and petrol tins of its own.) Then when supply columns have been sent up to units which have given a reliable map reference, too often such convoys run into the enemy before they can reach their destination; or having reached the map reference, they find no one there; or having found someone, they arrive in the middle of a battle, or of a hasty withdrawal. All this adds up to a hundred nightmares for the hard-working 'Q' service, and that they continue to function efficiently is a supreme tribute to their patience and endurance."

* * * * *

After the withdrawal from Benghazi 4th Indian Division was dispersed, with 5 Brigade sent to Palestine to prepare defences on the border with Syria, 7 Brigade given a similar task in Cyprus, and 11 Brigade despatched to the Canal Zone to train in Combined Operations. After a peaceful few weeks in the spring and early summer of 1942, during which there were changes of some units and personalities in the Division, 11 Brigade returned to the fray on the perimeter of Tobruk. The Brigade now comprised 2 Camerons, 2/5 Mahrattas, 2/7 Gurkhas and 25 Field Regiment. In the third week of June it was clear that Rommel was mounting a major assault on Tobruk. 11 Brigade put up splendid resistance but the Fortress Commander (the commander of 2nd South African Division), believing the situation to be hopeless, surrendered Tobruk. This meant the loss of 11 Brigade to 4th Indian Division but there were many escape stories. The Official History records the brief examples which follow.

Four officers and 60 gunners of 25 Field Regiment walked 400 miles as a formed body. Two havildars and three Gurkha riflemen rejoined the 8th Army at El Alamein; one of the havildars riding a camel which he had hired from some Arabs.

2/7th Gurkhas also provided the heroes of the following story told by the Assistant Military Secretary GHQ Middle East.

"One morning soon after the fall of Tobruk, three young officers of 2/7 Gurkhas, who were at the reinforcement camp, asked for an urgent appointment. The AMS saw them and estimated their combined service at 18 months. They requested that they should be allowed to form a new battalion of 2/7 Gurkha Rifles to take part in the re-capture of Tobruk. They quoted as precedent the First Great War when the Second Battalion was taken at Kut-el-Amara and the newly raised unit was in the force which eventually regained the Turkish stronghold. The AMS was so impressed with the young officers' earnestness that he recommended to GHQ India, that their request be granted. The officers were 2/Lieuts Clay, Tait and Taylor."

Rommel's drive for Egypt surged forward, and formations and units of the 8th Army in large and small groups delayed and harried as best they could, while withdrawing through various untenable positions until they reached the Ruweisat Ridge and El Alamein. There the coastal flank was held by 1st South African Division and the New Zealanders held the desert flank along the cliffs of the Qattara Depression: in between, the Ruweisat Ridge was the key and was already at risk. Before the defences there could be properly organised the Brigade endeavouring to do so was overrun by Rommel's armour. The enterprise which prevented Rommel from splitting the Alamein position at Ruweisat was the action of ROBCOL. *The broader picture is first drawn by the official history of the Division, then described in well-remembered detail by a senior subaltern of 83/85 Battery in 11 Field Regiment.*

The long association destined to ensue permits the story of 11 Field Regiment (Lieut-Colonel A. O. McCarthy MC) at El Alamein to be incorporated in this collection. At the outbreak of war these gunners had been stationed at Meerut, where under the leadership of Lieut-Colonel B. J. Fowler they had already established an outstanding reputation. They accompanied 8th Indian Division to the Persian Gulf. On 15th June when in Northern Iraq, 11 Field Regiment received orders for Western Desert. It covered 1,500 miles in 11 days and marched straight into the melee at Mersa Matruh. After an exciting disengagement Lieut-Colonel McCarthy and his men found their way back to El Alamein, picking up enough straggling guns to repair their losses. On 1st July, strong and fresh, they hurried forward with C Company of 1/4 Essex to form ROBCOL under Brigadier R. P. Waller, CRA, 10th Indian Division, and to dispute the passage of the Panzers across the rocky saddle-back of all-important high ground.

Shortly after 1000 hours on 2nd July, from a position near the tip of the ridge, 11 Field Regiment began to hammer masses of enemy transport in the Deir el Shein area. A German lorried infantry group threw in a quick attack, apparently to test the strength of the blocking forces. Enemy artillery found the range and searched the crest of the ridge.

The Panzers followed forward to mount the high ground. They were beaten back. As they swung to flank, the steady fire of the 25-pounders followed them. The Essex in their covering positions sat tight all day under a continuous bombardment. Casualties mounted. By nightfall seven guns had been knocked out and ammunition was all but exhausted. But for the first time since Tobruk, Rommel's armour had broken off action and had retired into the west.

Early next morning ROBCOL thrust forward to Point 97, where Ruweisat merges into the desert plain. A furious artillery battle raged throughout the forenoon; the Panzers took a mauling whenever they attempted to close. That afternoon, guns of the Royal Horse Artillery stiffened the blocking force. Lieut-Colonel Noble brought forward a composite rifle company and the Essex carrier platoon. Thereafter supporting arms hourly reached ROBCOL. It became WALCOL and continued to carry the battle to the enemy. Elements of 1 Armoured Division arrived, blocked the gaps on either side and gave firm flanks to the force holding the ridge. Furious gun duels and tank combats continued, but the crisis had passed. Afrika Korps had foundered against the rock of Ruweisat.

Slightly to the south of the main ridge, Lieut-Colonel Noble and his men found a wrinkle of high ground, named it Essex Ridge and prepared to live up to General Auchinleck's exhortation to harass the enemy without ceasing. In the next week they blew up a gun position, killing nine Germans, raided and burnt an enemy leaguer, captured some stray transport and took prisoners. Deploying his full force, Rommel endeavoured to by-pass the New Zealanders in the south. Thwarted in this attempt, he shifted his attack and struck at the South Africans on the seashore. Again he took a beating. As a war correspondent put it, "The Alamein line, fluid one day, elastic the next, in one short week became an iron wall against which the invaders battered in vain".

* * * * *

The Inside Story

Just before sunset on 1st July 1942 Rommel broke through the Alamein line, his tanks had overwhelmed the gallant defence of the 18th Indian Infantry Brigade in the Deir el Shein, at the foot of the Ruweisat Ridge which commands the whole area between the high ground round Alamein and the Qattara Depression. At that moment, and for the next 12 hours, there was no further organised defence between the spearhead of the Afrika Korps and Alexandria, which they expected to enter in a few hours. In Cairo, the day before, black clouds of smoke from burning files showed that many people believed Rommel would not stop short of the Suez Canal, his stated objective. But on 3rd July 1942, at 2256 hours – only 48 hours after his original breakthrough – he called off his attack and ordered his troops to dig in where they stood. The Delta was saved.

The crisis came on 2nd July 1942 at about the hour of the "sundowner" as nine guns of 83/85 Field Battery of 11 Field Regiment RA met the oncoming Afrika Korps on Ruweisat Ridge and, for the first time in many days, their advance was stopped.

To the north, the South African Division covered an immense area from the half-constructed box at Alamein down to the ridge itself. To the south were the New Zealanders and some weak mobile columns from 5th Indian Division, but though the New Zealand artillery fired many rounds that afternoon, they could only make their contribution at extreme range and were not directly engaged in the critical battle. The South Africans were fighting off an attack by 90 Light Division on their coastal box. On their left flank, however, they gave ground which for a time exposed the right flank of 11 Field Regiment.

On the ridge itself were elements of 1 Armoured Division (4 Armoured Brigade and 22 Armoured Brigade) and 50 Division. Again, the artillery of 1 Armoured Division took part in long-range exchanges. In the early evening they moved forward and, by closing the range, forestalled the enemy's attempt to outflank the forward guns. But there was little the armour could do to help; the few remaining Grants were under orders not to get engaged though a dozen Honeys made a brave sortie across our front in the late afternoon.

HQ 50 Division were trying to form three battle groups around the guns which had managed to get back in the break-out from Matruh. Of these only ROBCOL was ready at first light on 2nd July, and it was this unit that moved along the southern crest of Ruweisat in the direct line of the Afrika Korps' advance. It had been assembled by Brigadier Claude Eastman, CRA 50 Division, and was commanded by Brigadier "Rob" Waller, CRA 10th Indian Division. Its main artillery, 11 Field Regiment, had a few days before been part of 8th Indian Division in the north of Iraq, 1,500 miles away. During the action, command passed from 50 Division to 1 Armoured Division. Both Divisions were in 30 Corps and at 1415 hours 2nd July, 13 Corps took over. Small wonder that ROBCOL's history is difficult to disentangle!

11 Field Regiment was commanded by Lieut-Colonel A. O. MacCarthy, who had recently taken over. It had brought the field guns of 78/84 Field Battery and 83/85 Field Battery from India, and had been joined just before the battle by 265 Anti-Tank Battery. Four Bofors of 155 LAA (or possibly 113 LAA) Battery were also in the column.

78/84 Field Battery arrived on Ruweisat in good shape. It was commanded by the late Major John Ashton and, under him, it wrote its page of history on Ruweisat on 3rd July. It was certainly no idle spectator on 2nd July, but fate willed that 83/85 Field Battery with one troop of 265 Anti-Tank Battery and C Company, 1/4 Essex should lie in the direct line of the Afrika Korps' advance. 83/85 Field Battery just managed to slam the door in the face of the advancing enemy. 78/84 Field Battery next day managed to thrust home the bolt which made it secure; and by 3rd July, there was more cohesion to the British resistance. On 2nd July, Rommel could have broken through by silencing nine guns – and as darkness fell only one of the nine guns was still capable of effective fire! But, by that time, the Panzers were down to 26 runners.

Around the nine guns, were, in addition to the AA and Anti-Tank guns, the infantry; some machine guns of the Northumberland Fusiliers, some Essex Yeomanry, elements of the Guides Cavalry and even some 2/3 Gurkhas from 18 Indian Infantry Brigade who refused to leave the battle-field after the fall of their box in the Deir el Shein. To concentrate on the 25-prs is not to belittle the part which everyone played – it is a simple recognition of the fact that when a force of Mark IIIs and Mark IVs advances over desert terrain they can only be stopped by a major obstacle (which did not exist) or by guns of a sufficiently heavy calibre. 265 Anti-Tank Battery, minus a troop, were equipped with 2-prs and some 6-prs, which the Adjutant had picked up during the night of 30th June/1st July. This is perhaps a convenient place to record that in the early evening Major Geoff Armstrong brought up six guns of A Battery RHA and they joined in by firing 600 rounds and by filling the gap on our right flank.

The roll-call of 83/85 Field Battery, whose guns are the centre of this story, showed many differences on 2nd July from the well-knit unit which left Iraq less than 3 weeks before. The four guns of D Troop had not changed and they were served by men who had for the most part come with them from India, but three guns of E Troop had got stuck in a Wadi during the night break-out from Matruh (where they fought the enemy over open sights before they were overwhelmed). On 2nd July, E Troop had five guns, of which four were new to the Battery, surviving from three Indian Divisions which had been cut to pieces in the cauldron, at Sidi Rezegh and in the Deir el Shein. They had changed formations so many times that they are difficult to identify, but their original loyalties seem to have been to 32, 121, and 157 Field Regiments. Three of them were commanded by Sergeants Keelan, Wilkinson and Franklyn who, like Bombardier Lang, No 1 of the surviving E Troop Gun, all subsequently became BSMs in the regiment. The Battery Commander of 83/85, Major

J. M. Douglas, had had little chance of getting to know his new command. He had joined the battery at Mosul on 7th June and the order to march had come through a couple of days later. The Battery Captain, Captain E. J. S. Foster, arrived with Lieut A. M. MacGregor and 2nd Lieut P. Curry on 1st July. Curry and MacGregor joined Lieut Slight in E Troop. Slight and MacGregor were among the seven officers in 83/85 Battery wounded on 2nd July as were both the Troop Commanders (Captains Clements and Boyd). The battery suffered 100 casualties that day and on 3rd July its ration strength was down to seven officers (including three wounded) and 87 gunners. The same day the one serviceable gun went, under Sergeant Wilkinson, to join in 78/84 Battery's battle. By mid-afternoon three more guns were made ready for action and, for the next few days, 83/85 Battery fought as a troop of XI HAC, which was also under command of 11 Field Regiment. Finally the regiment remained in action on Ruweisat Ridge with only a three-day break, from 2nd July to 2nd November.

After the ROBCOL *action Ruweisat Ridge continued to be held against repeated attacks by Rommel and for a month 5 Brigade was part of the mixed force that achieved this, aggressive, defence. 11 Field Regiment was there too, shortly to join 4th Indian Division formally as opposed to having become an "honorary member"! At the end of August the battle of Alam Halfa was joined when Rommel looked forward to being in Alexandria in three days. The attack was again held and in the first week of September 4th Indian Division was at last reconstituted with 5 Brigade and 7 Brigade and relieved 5th Indian Division on the Ruweisat position. 161 Infantry Brigade was a third brigade under command temporarily taking the place of 11 Brigade. The Division at Alamein was constituted as follows:*

5th Indian Infantry Brigade
 1/4 Essex Regiment
 4/6 Rajputana Rifles
 3/10 Baluch Regiment
 Machine Gun Battalion 6 Rajputana Rifles

7th Indian Infantry Brigade
 1 Royal Sussex Regiment
 4/16 Punjab Regiment
 1/2 Goorkha Rifles

Divisional Artillery
  1 Field Regiment RA
  11 Field Regiment RA
  31 Field Regiment RA
  149 Anti-Tank Regiment RA
  57 Light Anti-Aircraft Regiment RA

The Divisional Artillery is specifically mentioned here because, as the Divisional history says:
  "No one in Fourth Indian Division would wish to make extravagant claims, but there is a sound basis for considering the Division's chief contribution to the winning of the war to have been the services rendered by the Divisional gunners in the elaboration and perfection of the new artillery technique. Certainly Fourth Indian Division led the way in the Eighth Army. Brigadier Dimoline afterwards carried his methods to Fourteenth Army in Burma."

There is in the Divisional History a graphic illustration of the justification for this claim contained in the following account by an Indian Army Public Relations Officer of the break-out from Alamein (Operation SUPERCHARGE*).*

THE BREAK-OUT

"At 0230 hours the guns began to bark and cough. Battery after battery registered with intermittent harassing fire. It was like the tuning up of a multi-engined bomber – warm up one engine, switch it off, try another, race one a bit, try two at a time, try one pair, both pairs. Until 0330 hours, everything was switched on with a rush and a deafening roar, which for an instant pinned the men to the ground. Then plain as day, looming before them, 5 Brigade saw the Wedge.

"It looked like a cloud that had suddenly risen out of a fissure in the earth, a steady and constant thickness of smoke and dust, where 400 guns cast their shells, one gun to every two yards of ground. It was a cataract of steel which poured out of the air, churning the earth into powder. Down each side fireworks ran – Bofors guns firing tracer as flank guides. Minute by minute the crescendo heightened and deepened until at 0400 hours, slowly, inexorably, like a machine when power surges into its dead metal, the Wedge began to move. The drive had begun.

"The men who led this advance told me that in that thirty minutes while they waited for the curtain of steel to be woven, there came to them a wonderful feeling of confidence. The Wedge was so exact that they felt the barrage to be part of themselves; a weapon in their hands; as an airman feels when the earth has slipped away from him, when his engines beat sweet and true and he knows he has great power within his grasp. The Indians moved forward not as men ahead of guns, but as men behind a shield. They were the garrison, the crew of the Wedge. They moved freely without fear. 'They could have leaned against it', said their Brigadier. The first casualties, and indeed most of the casualties, were men who followed the wall of shell so closely that they became queasy from the fumes of our explosives.

"Of fighting there was little. It was more tidying-up – winkling out the dazed occupants of dug-out and dusting off slit trenches where a few panzer grenadiers sought to sell their lives dearly. There were incidents, of course. While a German stood in a dug-out entrance with his hands raised, another crept up behind him and drew a bead on a Rajputan Rifle Officer. When a subedar collared the marksman, the irate Englishman laid into the German with his fists. The subedar saw the Wedge marching on without them, and spoke to his officer with some such words as 'See, Sahib, there is our battle. Let us go on with it'. Every now and then desperate enemies, who had come unscathed through the torrent of steel, sprang up and sought to fight. Sudden deadly clashes occurred. A havildar whom the Rajputana Rifles mourn took a mortal wound in dealing single-handed with a dozen Germans. But ahead the men marched steadily with the Wedge, 35 yards in each minute, moving without hurt over ground which every device of war had made deadly. And so perfectly was the Wedge planned, that when our men had passed beyond the range of field guns, and the mediums and heavies took up the task, those who followed a stone's throw from the curtain of fire saw no gap or break in it.

"I asked a young officer of the Essex how it felt to walk forward for nearly three hours with a storm of 400 guns beating about his head, and their shells blasting a trail a few yards before his feet. 'Engrossing', he said, 'but after a while, it seemed a bit lonely. I was rather pleased when, a little before dawn, I saw some shapes in the gloom, and realised that we had somebody with us'.

"These shapes were the tank screen – South Africans and the Royals in their armoured cars. The Wedge was all but driven. At the first streak of light in the east, the infantry came into broken ground. They saw before them the kidney-shaped contour which they had been shown on the map. The guns lifted and were done; there was quiet but for the crackle of small arms fire. Out in front little figures scuttled madly, seeking holes. A carrier platoon went out to bring them in. Then another noise, thunder out of the east, and more thunder. The roar mounted. The tanks came plunging through – hundreds of tanks, lunging to the west through the gap the Wedge had made, and wheeling north for the kill. The sun rose on the last of Alamein."

With the break-out and pursuit of the Axis force from El Alamein came the fate which the members of 4th Indian Division had met on previous occasions and disliked intensely: the clearing up of the battlefield and the break-up of the Division into individual units and groups with differing tasks. Some Indian formation commanders put forward their objections strongly to the Army Commander, and gained some sympathy from General Montgomery who, as a matter of principle believed in the use of properly balanced formations under their own commanders.

While other, luckier formations pressed Rommel from one lay-back position to another, Generaal Tuker continued to fight for the return of units to the Division and its reassembly as a complete fighting formation.

Eighth Army's pursuit to Tripoli had to be accelerated to ensure coordination with the North African operations of 1st Army and the Americans. The pursuing troops had over-extended lines of communication. Rommel had fallen back to the very strong Mareth position and had to counter-attack from this rapidly if he was to prevent the 8th Army opening up the Port of Tripoli and reaching full strength in supplies as well as formations.

The reconstituted 4th Indian Division was given the task of outflanking the Mareth Line through minefields and defended passes until poised above the Gabes plain. With 4th Indian Division about to fall on his rear and 1st Armoured Division breaking through on the opposite flank, Rommel once again skilfully disengaged and fell back to Wadi Akarit.

The initial plan for the 8th Army assault on the Wadi Akarit was subsequently modified as a result of representations from General Tuker. The eventual plan was for 51st Highland Division and 50th Division to make an 0430 direct assault on Rommel's position near the coast while 7 Brigade seized the wildly jagged peaks of Fatnassa and 5 Brigade went through. The 4th Division attack started silently as soon as darkness fell, before the frontal assault started.

A Vignette of 1st/2nd Gurkhas Before Wadi Akarit

General Tuker explained his plan for the Wadi Akarit battle in a small dry wadi to the Battalion and Regimental commanders or their representatives. 1/2 Gurkhas were to lead the silent night attack. It was a daring plan in extremely difficult terrain and, in an earlier discussion with Brigadier Lovett, the Brigade Commander, General Tuker, had quoted Adam Lindsay Gordon's advice on tricky fences:

"Look before you leap,
But, if you mean leaping, don't look long,
For the weakest fence will then grow stiff
And the stiffest, doubly strong."

At the end of the briefing there came the usual synchronisation of watches and "Any Questions". The question from the officer from 1/2 Gurkhas said everything about that Battalion. He sprang smartly to attention and asked "One prisoner for identification, Sahib, as usual?"

*　　*　　*　　*　　*

With 4th/16th Punjabis at Wadi Akarit

In this battle the main 8th Army attack was to go in on the right flank – at dawn. During the night the 4th Indian Division was to be put in a diversionary silent attack on to the Zouai feature.

That night 7 Brigade formed up, on foot, with 1/2 Gurkha Rifles leading and the 4/16 on the left. Every man could see his neighbour to the side and front. Two-thousand odd men then moved forward *en masse*, feeling their way in the pitch dark. The Gurkhas achieved their objective silently and I was then sent for by the CO and ordered to creep forward with B Company and take a ridge which showed up as a silhouette on the sky line. sky line.

I returned the few yards to my Company who were all kneeling "at the ready" and gave the whispered signal to "rise up". And that was the end of the silent attack! Like one man B Company rose up and charged forward shouting "Maro, Maro, Hadzri" at the top of their voices. I had no option but to be carried along with them and after 300 yards or so we swept up a ridge and took it.

When dawn came another ridge appeared to our front from which enemy fire was coming. Once again, but this time on orders, B Company charged forward with fixed bayonets and captured the ridge, taking 300 prisoners.

From this ridge a valley stretched out to the north and in this enemy were seen. I ordered Platoon Havildar Mohammed Aslam to take his platoon and round them up – but not to go too far. He set off with the platoon and Havildar Mohammed Azam. After a while I saw the platoon advancing across the valley, turn west across the road, then in open formation, return to attack another strongly held feature. I could not stop them from that distance and all we could do was to give supporting fire. What a sight! Twenty-five men attacking a high hill, studded with enemy trenches. The sheer audacity of it surprised and frightened the defenders who, as the platoon approached, threw down their arms and surrendered – 300 or more of them.

*   *   *   *   *

On the lighter side there is an equally typical story from 1/2 Goorka Rifles:

An Order is an Order

By and large in the long haul from Alamein to Tunis the NAAFI did its stuff pretty well, and our Officer's Mess was kept fairly well stocked with that most needful commodity Scotch Whisky. Inevitably, however, there were occasions when communications broke down, our indents were unanswered and stocks began to run low. On one such occasion the PMC gave an order to the Mess Havildar that officers were not to take away bottles of Scotch from the Mess: they could have only half a bottle. Shortly after this things brightened up, all our past indents came through and the Mess tent was stacked with cases of Scotch.

A few days later I wanted to give a small party in my tent to some particular friends and I sent my Gurkha orderly over to the Mess for a bottle of Scotch. He returned, and something like the following dialogue ensued:

Orderly: The Mess Havildar says officers are not allowed to take bottled of Scotch from the Mess to their tents.

Self: I know there was such an order, but that was when we were short. Now there are masses of the stuff.

Orderly: Well you'd better see the Mess Havildar yourself. He's a Havildar; I'm a Rifleman. You can argue with him; I can't.

Accordingly over to the Mess tent I went to see the Mess Havildar who was a great friend of mine as indeed he was with everyone. Talk went as follows:

Self: Now then Ambahadur, what's all this about not being able to get a bottle of Scotch!

Ambahadur: Sorry Sahib. Major Sahib's hukm.

Self: Yes I know, but that was when we were short. Now we've tons of the stuff.

Ambahadur: Sorry Sahib. The hukm has not been cancelled.

Self: Where's the Major Sahib. I'll go and see him myself.

Ambahadur: Sorry Sahib. He's gone to dine with the gora paltan (Royal Sussex).

Self: Oh dear! Well, can I have half a bottle?

Ambahadur: O yes, Sahib, certainly!

Self: Can I have two half bottles?

Ambahadur: O yes, Sahib, certainly!

And he solemnly opened a full bottle, measured out 10 tots – or whatever it was – into an empty bottle and then another 10 tots. The first bottle was now empty and the second bottle full. I asked "Wouldn't it have been quicker just to have given me the first bottle?" He replied, "I don't know anything about that Sahib, but an order is an order."

The Gurkha, when he wants to, and he often does, can present an inscrutable face, but I'm sure I detected then a twinkle in those friendly almond eyes.

With the battle over at Wadi Akarit, Rommel's last bastion facing the 8th Army was the ground between Enfidaville on the coast and the mountains around Djebel Garci about 20 miles inland. For the attempt to "bounce" the Axis forces off this position before it could become a thoroughly organised defensive barrier, Field Marshal Montgomery had 10th Corps comprising 7th Armoured Division, 2nd New Zealand Division, 4th Indian Division and 50th Division. As was not unknown, however, the picture of a loosely occupied area out of which the enemy could be "bounced" without too much difficulty, proved to be based upon optimistic intelligence assessments. The battle for Djebel Garci and Enfidaville proved to involve some of the most desperate fighting of the campaign.

GARCI AND ENFIDAVILLE

AN ACCOUNT BY A JEMADAR OF 1/9 GURKHA RIFLES

"I was challenged in a foreign language. I felt it was not the British language or I would have recognised it. To make quite sure I crept up and found myself looking into the face of a German. I recognised him by his helmet. He was fumbling with his weapon so I cut off his head with my kukri. Another appeared from a slit trench and I cut him down also. I was able to do the same to two others, but one made a great deal of noise, which raised the alarm. I had a cut at a fifth but I am afraid I only wounded him. Yet perhaps the wound was severe, for I struck him between the neck and the shoulder.

"I was now involved in a struggle with a number of Germans, and eventually, after my hands had become cut and slippery with blood, they managed to wrest my kukri from me. One German beat me over the head with it, inflicting a number of wounds. He was not very skilful, however, sometimes striking me with the sharp edge but oftener with the blunt.

"They managed to beat me to the ground where I lay pretending to be dead. The Germans got back into their trenches and after a while I looked up. I could not see anything for my eyes were full of blood. I wiped the blood out of my eyes and quite near I saw a German machine-gun. I thought, 'If only I can reach that gun I shall be able to kill the lot.' By now it was getting light and as I lay thinking of a plan to reach the gun, my platoon advanced and started to hurl grenades among the enemy. But they were also falling very near me, so I thought that if I did not move I really would be dead. I managed to get to my feet, and ran towards my platoon. Not recognising me, I heard one of my men call, 'Here comes the enemy! Shoot him!' I bade them not to do so. They recognised my voice and let me come in.

"My hands being cut about and bloody, and having lost my kukri, I had to ask one of my platoon to take my pistol out of my holster and to put it in my hand. I then took command of my platoon again.

"I met my company commander, who bade me go to the Regimental Aid Post. I said, 'Sahib, there is fighting to be done, and I know the enemy's dispositions. I must stay and command my platoon.' But he firmly ordered me and I had to go. Yet before I went, one of my Bren gunners was hit, and my company commander, although wounded in the neck, took over the Bren gun and continued to fire it. Moreover, the doctor sahib, having bandaged me, refused to allow me to return to my platoon."

A FIELD AMBULANCE PICTURE

"There had not been a minute's rest for twenty hours. Mazhar and I decided to run the night ADS so that Chaudhari and Willson could start again fresh in the morning. The stream of cases continued until midnight. Pictures come to mind of a constant stream of people. The medical corporal of the Essex scrounging tea with sugar; a visiting Colonel wounded while watching the battle; a Gunner Brigadier asking about the shelling; a boy Gurkha proudly displaying his blooded kukri; a wounded B.O.R. blasted into near coma; constant visitors asking news of friends. Stretcher-bearers arriving exhausted with hands bleeding; reliefs sent up, young Madrassis yet to prove themselves. Dawn showed that the strain was telling. The Brigadier looked ten years older and the Brigade Major was grey from lack of sleep. Captain Holman was ordered back to get desperately needed rest, but he returned later to finish the job he had so magnificently done. Only arrest would have stopped him. We heard later that he had put out a fire on an ammunition dump. One can be truly thankful that such medical officers as he were spared, for God knows they are needed."

* * * * *

Two Accounts of the Defeat of a Counter-attack by True Professionals

FROM THE OFFICIAL HISTORY

"On the night of April 29th the Londoners seized Point 130. Early next morning a quick thrust hurled them from the high ground. No reserve position had been organised, and the enemy followed up the withdrawal, driving vigorously on Enfidaville. The heavy concentration of field regiments was covered by the deployment of 7 Brigade along the borders of the olive groves, with 1/2 Gurkha Rifles and 4/16 Punjabis in the forward zone. The latter battalion was engrossed with plans for the Tebaga attack and all officers of the Gurkhas except Captain M. A. Ormsby were absent on conference. The enemy was within 2,000 yards of the leading wave of field guns when the alarm was sounded. Delay and confusion might have been expected. Instead, Punjabis and Gurkhas reacted with precision and assurance. Riflemen took charge of sections, NCOs of companies, and the covering troops doubled forward to contact the enemy and to pin him down. What might have been a serious situation was averted by alertness and battle-readiness."

AND FROM 4/16 PUNJABIS

"The highly successful silent night attack at Wadi Akarit by 7 Indian Infantry Brigade was perhaps the classic example of the pitch of training reached by British and Indian soldiers alike, but the following account underlines this particularly as far as the junior ranks were concerned. On 29th April the Battalion was at a concentration area in an olive grove behind Enfidaville. The previous night, a Division, having just arrived direct from Paiforce after one of the longest approach marches in history, had been launched into their first encounter with the enemy. A swift dawn thrust hurled them back in some disarray through the lines of the 4/16 Punjabis and 1/2 Gurkhas. The situation was serious. The enemy were within 2000 yards of the guns which had been deployed well forward. Officers and VCO's of the two regiments were engrossed in conference behind the position. Instinctively, Havildars and Naiks took charge of companies and platoons and sepoys of sections. Groups doubled forward, made contact with the enemy and pinned them down with fire, thus avoiding a possible debacle by battle-readiness and alertness."

*   *   *   *   *

While Enfidaville still held out a strategic decision was being made, and on 30th April at 1100 hours signals were despatched. Some paragraphs from The Tiger Kills *cogently describe some moments in 4th Indian Division's part in the end in Africa.*

Towards the End in Africa

The 4th Indian Division, the 7th Armoured Division, and the 201st Guards Brigade, would leave the Army which had been built about them, and would take the roads to central Tunisia for the final stroke of the North African campaign.

Four hours after receiving his message, the 4th Indian Division was on the line of march. It is eloquent of the degree of organisation that the 8th Army achieved that divisions numbering many thousand men, and thousands of vehicles, could at four hours notice leave for another part of Africa, two hundred miles away without confusion or delay. It is seldom in this story that the opportunity has offered to pay a tribute to the hardworking transport companies which have borne the fighting men from one end of Africa to another. When it is remembered that tyres do not grow on camel thorn, and that no springs or half-shafts have been made which will endure desert potholes and boulders indefinitely, it is realised what a splendid task has been performed unobtrusively by the recovery sections, the various line workshops, and the many other services manned by the officers and men of the IEME and REME. On this occasion as always, the transport services did not fail. Taking station along the two hundred miles of unknown mountain road they nursed the long convoys through, and theirs was no small contribution to the victory to come.

When night fell on 30th April, a steady stream of Divisional vehicles was passing through the holy city of Kairouan, and were taking the long southern route to Sbeitla, where the ruins of the old Roman cities still stand. Headlights were allowed, but after years of black-out not one vehicle in a hundred had bulbs. Driving steadily through the night at a regulated pace, they passed Sheiba and came into the fertile valleys of central Tunisia, with trim tidy crops mounting to the hill crests, neat villages reminiscent of the Midi, girt about with almond and fruit orchards or with rich pasture land in which contented sheep continued to graze as the unending convoys passed them.

After a short halt for a "brew-up" at dawn, the traffic flowed on, quickening to day pace. The Division was now in new country, filled with civilians who stood along the road, thrusting up their finger in the "V" sign, while children wearing berets raced beside the trucks shouting in voluble French to the uncomprehending jawans, who twirled their moustaches and examined the cattle and sheep in pasture with deep interest. Then scuttle-helmeted Americans began to line the roads. The bearded Sikhs in their pugarees, the Rajputs, Jats, Punjabi Mussulmans, and squat little Gurkhas were something new to them. The Americans gave the "thumbs-up" sign, and friendly jests crackled as the lorries lumbered past. So throughout the day, up the long valley from Le Kef to Le Krib, through the Provencal town of Teboursouk on its hillside, and past the great monastery of the white fathers at Thibar, the 4th Division drew nearer to the bastion which the enemy defended so desperately in the fortress of Tunisia – the Medjez-el-Bab gateway into the open plains of Tunis.

Here the British 1st Army was met. The contrast was extreme. With their new vehicles, camouflaged in dark colours to blend with the trees and fields, this other Army might have belonged to another nation. Into this ordered scene swept the battered old trucks of the 8th Army, painted a light sandy grey, with never a windscreen, rarely a hood and mudguards tied on with bits of wire; scratched rusty veterans of an advance of two thousand miles.

The battle had reached its last stage, and the enemy's line distended by terrific hammering was almost ready to break. But along the left of Medjez-el-Bab–Tunis road, a group of features still supplied him with sufficient cover to organise an effective defence, and to deny the gateway to the British tanks. On the left front the 1st British Division was involved in savage fighting among the broken ground of the Bou Huaker. On its right, the 4th British Division faced the village of Montuarnaud, whose distillery was a landmark. Between these two objectives a small valley lay, with rugged foothills running to the north-east. The plan of battle called for the 4th Indian Division to crash through between the two British Divisions, and to reach the open plain some 4 miles ahead. Six objectives were set down, two of which were to be taken by the 5th Brigade, who then would be leap-frogged by 7th Brigade. Thereafter an Army Tank Brigade, under command of the 4th Indian Division, would over-run the final objectives. Then the 7th British Armoured Division would pass through. Thus were the two Divisions, which had been in Africa since the beginning, selected to make the end.

The attack was set down for the morning of 5th May, and days of busy planning followed the arrival of the reinforcements from the 8th Army. The 4th Indian Division learned that its fame had preceded it, and that 1st Army commanders were anxious to know its views on hill fighting. General Tuker asked for a night attack instead of a dawn assault, and it was given him. After reports had been submitted on the terrific effects of artillery concentrations at Garci and Akarit, the number of rounds per gun was doubled. A token barrage and concentration shoots were substituted for a straight barrage programme.

The conference with the Armoured Brigade likewise produced an interesting exchange of views. Going over the map, the tank commander said to General Tuker: "I take it that we go in there?" "No," said General Tuker, "that is where my infantry goes." "But naturally we go first," said the tank commander. "No," said General Tuker, "naturally we go first. You keep on stepping up in close support of the infantry. When we have opened the gate, you go through and keep on going. But you wil wait for us to show that the way is clear." When the battle was over, the tank commander returned to thank the 4th Indian Division for its magnificent co-operation.

THE END IN AFRICA

The surrender of all the Axis troops in Africa was accepted on 12th May and, appropriately, the Division was represented. The Tiger Kills *describes the events.*

Later in the morning, the Royal Sussex pushed into the St Marie du Zit area, taking more than 500 prisoners. While these were being rounded up, a German staff car flying a white flag arrived. Colonel Nolte of General Von Arnim's staff stepped out. He was bearer in a personal letter from Von Arnim to the General Officer Commanding the Allied troops in the area. The Royal Sussex Commander (Major Bryant) passed the emissaries through to Division Headquarters near Ain El Asker.

But before the surrender could be formalised, the 2nd Gurkhas, who had been mopping up from the other end of the valley, had taken a hand in it.

That morning they made contact with Frenchmen pushing north from Zaghouan. Colonel Showers, who led two companies on foot, had arrived at the bottom of the hill. While his men rested, he decided to climb to the top and see what was on the other side. His orderly, Rifleman Sarghana Limbu, accompanied him. From the crest of the hill he saw a German staff car and a German officer beside it waving a white flag. With Sarghana Limbu's tommy-gun at the ready, Colonel Showers went down the hill, turned the corner, and found nearly a thousand Germans forming up on parade. They were dressed in smart uniforms, clean shaven and boots polished, all spick and span. Colonel Showers afterwards admitted that he felt rather embarrassed as he walked through the ranks towards an imposing caravan. A high staff officer approached him and said that Colonel Nolte had already left to sue for terms of surrender. Colonel Showers, accompanied by a staff officer and a white flag bearer, proceeded in the German staff car towards his Brigade Headquarters. On the way they met Colonel Glennie returning to place a guard over Von Arnim's Headquarters. General Alfrey, commanding the 5th Corps, and General Tuker arrived soon after, and terms of capitulation were arranged.

Late that afternoon, General Von Arnim, Commander of all the Axis forces in Africa, emerged from his caravan. His staff had lined up, and gave a punctilious display of Prussian military etiquette. Von Arnim then entered an open car and stood Hitler fashion, acknowledging the salutes of his men, as he drove off with a Gurkha officer and a Royal Sussex guard. On his way he passed thousands of his own men also going into captivity. The 4th Division had no idea how many it had captured. After reaching 15,000 the count was given up.

BEFORE AND BETWEEN CAMPAIGNS

To many there was no doubt that the unique spirit of 4th Indian Division owed very much to the Division being lucky enough to be training together outside Cairo.

Most used to visit various "flesh pots" whenever possible: and got to know one another in the course of many, and varied, relaxing, hilarious, and sometimes bawdy occasions.

It could be said that affection was generated as between close friends of the same mind. It was natural, therefore, that when together in battle, there was an instinctive understanding and trust: sometimes there was no need even to communicate aloud; thoughts and wishes seemed to be followed by instinctive action.

Although this applied initially in 1939/40, and there were many, many changes among individuals, the same spirit and understanding seemed to be transferred as those who came later always were determined to live up to, or surpass the example of those who had set this pattern.

*   *   *   *   *

After the Division had been inspected by King George VI – the King Emperor on June 1943, it returned to the Nile Delta.

Alexandria had much to offer in the way of recreation and one of the stories of the 4/16 Punjabis concerns the anti-tank platoon. The platoon commander had been invited to a drink with a naval friend in the fashionable Cecil Hotel. He declined, saying that the platoon was waiting for him outside in Mohammed Ali Square; whereupon, his friend said that they should come too. Much to the surprise of the red-tabbed clientele, the jawans filed through the lounge and up the stairs in good order, regaled themselves with ample supplies of beer and departed in like manner; commenting most favourably on the excellence of inter-service co-operation.

*   *   *   *   *

46

The acquiring of the formidable black goat "Rastus" by 4/16 Punjabis has already been recorded. As the Battalion mascot he had picked up a voracious appetite for cigarettes. As this time, in order to use up stocks, NAAFI were insisting on a 50% issue of some extremely inferior cigarettes, inaptly named "Red Bird", whenever other brands were ordered.

By a stroke of genius the "Rastus Test" was devised. He resolutely refused to accept these cigarettes, rejecting them with disgust, but would immediately consume any other reasonable brand proffered. On the strength of this, Divisional Headquarters wre able to insist on "Red Bird" cigarettes being withdrawn from sale.

* * * * *

And Do You Remember...

... Being on leave from the desert and going to the Gezirah Club? Those Sunday lunches – those dangerous games of mixed hockey? Drinking Stella beer whilst watching the pretty girls swimming in the club pool?

... being called "George" by those fly-whisk vendors? Going to Tommy's bar? Those highly entertaining revues arranged by the civilians in Cairo and Alex – "The Blue Pencil Revue", Mrs Cyril Barker's concert parties?

... Madame Bardia's? or the cabaret acts at the Continental Hotel? Watching the multifarious uniforms go by while drinking gin on the verandah at Shepeards or the Continental? Enjoying the cool of the evening drinking Stella outside the Heliopolis Palace?

... how much our health and well-being and our morale depended on the talent, skill, devotedness and charm of the Nursing Services and VADs – on and off duty?

... those gharri races – usually against our New Zealand friends?

... that ball of fire "Wee Mac" (11th Field Regiment's A. O. McCarthy) dispensing Alka-Seltzers at an impossible hour of the morning after a monumental binge – with apparently the same bright gleam in his glass eye as his real one? His "Monday Morning" glass eye was alleged to be a matching bloodshot!

INTO EUROPE

The Division took ship for Italy from Alexandria in early December. The stokers of one ship went on strike in Alexandria and the drivers of 1st and 11th Field Regiments stoked in four-hour shifts. They reckoned that this counted as "light duties" compared with the unlimited hours which had been customary in the Western Desert.

Another illustration of the adaptability of the members of the Division of all races occurred in one of the MT ships during the passage. There were representatives of many regiments aboard and, inevitably therefore, the need for two "cookhouses" in addition to the ship's galley.

One day out from Alexandria, however, a small deputation asked to see the OC Troops. There were two cookhouses, two sets of equipment, two types of rations – but only one cook who really knew his job. Could they have permission to combine their resources? They could and they did; to everyone's satisfaction.

The unloading of the MT ships provided another glimpse of familiar characteristics: the cavalier fashion in which Johnny Gurkha tended to deal with his mechanical transport and his cheerful imperturbability.

On the quayside were some Gurkhas waiting to drive away their transport as it was unloaded. As always they were immaculate in battle order. A Jeep was hoisted out of the hold by a crane and deposited carefully on the quay facing inland, ready to drive away. The order was given and the little rifleman jumped smartly into the driver's seat. The engine started at a touch. The gear was engaged with that disdain of mechanism which can only really be displayed by a Gurkha soldier, and with an equally decisive pressure on the accelerator, the Jeep disappeared backwards into the harbour.

After what seemed to be a very long pause the rifleman reappeared, gasping but, inevitably soon grinning – if just a little shamefacedly – at the row of heads peering over the quayside. The Subedar Major concurrently brought about the removal of the grin from the face, and the Jeep from the depths; the former by a stream of Gurkhali, and the latter by the same crane that had so recently put the Jeep on the quayside. It was a picture and a story long to be remembered and did much at the time to lighten the first shock of the Italian winter in the Appennines.

The changes to which members of 4th Indian Division had to adapt very quickly were not only those of climate and terrain although these were drastic enough. It was not long before they were to compare movement of vehicles and heavy equipment through deep mud, with movement across the desert, and contrast trenches either shin-deep in water or inadequate scrapes in the rocks, with their desert equivalent; all to the detriment of the former, in spite of memories of bad going on occasions. From the climate and terrain aspects there were few that would argue against the Western Desert as a place to fight a war.

There was, however, another and much worse feature of the fighting in Italy. It was a place of towns, villages and farms. People were trying to continue to live, and work where they could, in the middle of a battle; and for very many of them, particularly in southern Italy, it was not their war.

A Field Battery Command Post was in a part of a small farmhouse not far from Lanciano. The farmer and his wife still lived on the premises; so did the three cows that the small-holding relied upon for its milk production.

The farm was on the reverse side of a hill. The valley contained several gun positions and was shelled regularly by German batteries; as they were in their turn. Casualties were inevitable, civilian as well as military.

Within the Command Post the arrival of two shells brought the accustomed effect of concussion, dust and flying fragments of all sorts. But with the accompanying checking of command post staff and equipment there came from the rear of the farmhouse a wailing which had become all too familiar in Italy. Someone had lost someone or something, or at least this was threatened.

The Battery Commander who had been on the spot and the Command Post Officer went to investigate.

One shell had hit the cow byre and the farmer and his wife were gazing at the wrecked building and, quite literally, wringing their hands and loudly lamenting. They could not be blamed. In a way they had virtually lost one of the family and an indispensable part of their meagre livelihood in one stroke. One of the three cows had been almost disembowelled by the shell and would certainly never give milk again. She was still alive though and in agony. While the Battery Commander drew his pistol, the Command Post Officer tried to explain – without any Italian – to the distraught farmer and his wife that since death was inevitable it was best that it be quick. Nevertheless the shot brought immediate renewed anguished voices from the desolate pair. Then it was back to the war.

This was the side of fighting in Europe that made it a much sadder, somehow less clean, business than it had been in the open spaces of the Western Desert.

The strange business of no longer fighting a war in an environment virtually empty of other than the protagonists and all their accoutrements, but in an environment shared with a population trying to maintain a life outside the war, was brought home to members of the Division in a multitude of ways; some more memorable than others.

Fifth Indian Brigade had had a long night's drive in convoy across the Appennines to the flatlands of the River Po. As dawn came 1/4 Essex drew into a small village just behind the front line. The Battalion stopped near a farmhouse on the outskirts of the village and waited for orders for deployment. Two soldiers, thinking that the farm had been deserted, went foraging, and a furious clucking soon accompanied a hectic chase of a hen round the yard. At that moment a window on the first floor was flung open, a woman's head appeared, and a totally unexpected English voice called out "––– off, and leave my ––– ing 'ens alone. We don't need no liberation 'ere."

* * * * *

Cassino

From a period of patrolling, probing attacks and slogging at close quarters in the mud on the Orsogna/Ortona line on the Eastern (8th Army) side of Italy, 4th Indian Division was switched to the 5th Army, closely following its old colleagues, 2nd New Zealand Division.

The task facing these two old friends and 78th (British) Division was to pass through the 34th and 36th US Divisions and capture Cassino.

The reality that 2nd New Zealand Corps found was the remnants of two divisions which had fought themselves to a standstill and had then grimly held on to the gains they had made at appalling cost: a cost that was being added to every hour they remained exposed to the fire power and uninterrupted observation from Monastery Hill.

It is doubtful if at this time there was a finer battle machine in the world than 4th Indian Division. Three years of incessant combat had hardened Britons and Indians alike into indomitable fighters, sensitive to the vagaries, instant to the necessities, of battle. The world heard much of them; Prime Minister Churchill paid them tribute in the Commons; the King-Emperor travelled to Tripoli to thank them in person, and to pin the Victoria Cross on Subedar Lalbahadur Thapa. Throughout that summer they rested and trained patiently, once again waiting for the call which never failed to come as the war mounted in vehemence. In December they crossed into Italy, and a month later took over a sector on the Adriatic coast. Here the mud, sleet and slush of abominable winter weather conditioned them for the ordeals to come.

The Division was again at full strength, for a reconstituted 11th Brigade comprised old comrades in a new 2 Camerons, a new 2/7 Gurkhas, and the 4/6 Rajputanas, which had been replaced in 5th Brigade by their 1/6 Battalion. On 1st February and Division began to move 65 miles to the south-west, across the Appennines, where nightly the sky was livid with flashes, and the thunder of the guns grew until the ground trembled with the shock of artillery. At the little town of Cassino, known to military scholars as a model of impregnable terrain, an American Corps, with gallantry beyond praise, had tried to storm the great fortress which barred the road to Rome. Isolated, frozen, battered by night and by day, handfuls of indomitable men clung to positions which they had clawed from the grip of the enemy. When the Indians relieved these great soldiers, brigades barely mustered 400 men. Of one battalion only 50 men remained, and they were so spent that they had to be carried out on stretchers.

Such was the fearful field to which 4th Indian Division was now committed. The desperate position in the Anzio bridge-head impelled High Command to brook no delay. Brigadier Lovett's 7th Brigade, inured to shock, was chosen to lead the way. The attack was planned to go in from the right flank, where the Americans had gained a footing on Snakes Head Ridge. Points 593 and 444 must be stormed before a start line could be established for assault on the main objective – the mighty massif of Monastery Hill.

Now came that proud and tragic six weeks in which, for the only time in the war, the inextinguishable ardour of "Jo Hukm" failed to vouchsafe victory. On the night of 14th February the Royal Sussex surged against Point 593, to encounter paratroopers who fought with unequalled fanaticism and disregard of death in foxholes and weapon pits hidden among the rocks. Thrown back, the same battalion attacked next night and stormed their objective but through some misunderstanding were recalled. On the night of 17th February, 1/2 Gurkhas, 1/9 Gurkhas, 4/6 Rajputanas, with the Rajputana Machine Gun Battalion in close support, came forward and flung themselves at the high ground. In a melee even fiercer than Garci, the Rajputanas took and lost Point 593. The Gurkha battalions were swept forward across minefields under an unparalleled blaze of mortar

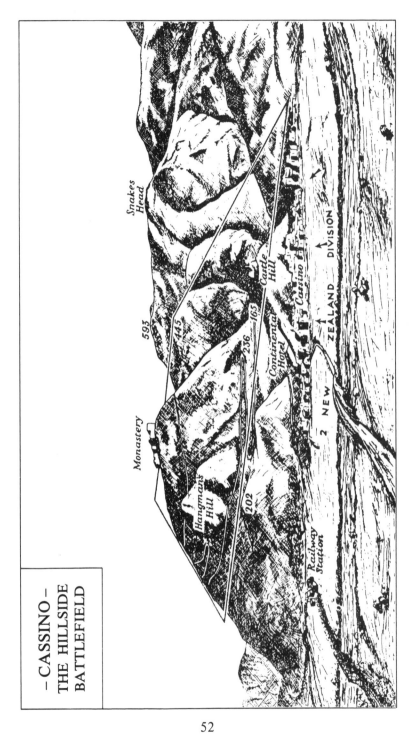

– CASSINO –
THE HILLSIDE
BATTLEFIELD

bombs, grenades and spandau fire, in a great bid to win the supreme prize of Monastery Hill. Two-thirds of 1/2 Gurkhas were down in 10 minutes yet the survivors battled on, leaving their dead far up on the slopes of the final objective. The attack failed, for the task was more than men born of women could encompass. Not only the infantry and artillery (11th Field Regiment in particular) paid toll in this maelstrom of battle; every service lost heavily. During the battle Subedar Subramanyan, a Madrassi sapper, covered a mine with his body to save his comrades and posthumously received the George Cross.

It was 15th March before a second attack could be mounted. On that date 5th Brigade, together with the New Zealand Division, attempted to reach Monastery Hill by first clearng the town of Cassino which lay, a heap of broken masonry, in the shadow of the great fortress. Once again fighting rose to a crescendo of unbelievable bitterness. The Essex held Castle Hill, while 1/6 Rajputanas joined the Kiwis in bitter and fluctuating fighting on the lower slopes. Two nights later 1/9 Gurkhas won imperishable fame in one of the greatest exploits of the war. They stormed Hangman's Hill and for seven days and nights beat off the enemies who had closed in a ring around them. Those who lived were finally withdrawn when the operation was abandoned as hopeless.

* * * * *

4th Indian's Balaclava

The Battle of Cassino was one of those great and tragic occasions when indomitable antagonists meet in a herculean clash in which fortune decides the victor; but where, in justice, there should be no loser.

The history of 4th Indian Division describes the plan for the first assault as follows:

"All the resources of Fourth Indian Division would be thrown into an assault *a outrance* and 2 New Zealand Division simultaneously would attack on a separate front. The new plan called for 4/6 Rajputana Rifles with three companies of Royal Sussex under command to put an end to resistance on Point 593 and thereafter to strike downwards along the ridge to Point 444 in the rear of the Monastery. Two hours later, 1/2 and 1/9 Gurkhas would smash through on the left of the opening assault and storm the Monastery. Thereafter they would exploit downhill to the south of Cassino town until Highway 6 had been brought under fire.

Concurrently 2 New Zealand Division would force the lower Rapido and drive for the entrance of the Liri valley, where contact would be effected with the Gurkhas. 1/4 Essex and 1/6 Rajputana Rifles of 5 Brigade would move to the attack on the north of Cassino town, thus pinning its defenders between two fires. The uncommitted battalions, 2 Camerons and 2/7 Gurkha Rifles, would supply porters and support companies for the assault groups."

The history also provides as good a summary as exists of the individual and collective gallantry that took place on that night of chaos and killing when almost the only element of 4th Indian thrown into the combat which survived unscathed was its spirit.

"The enemy swept the approach with harassing shoots, causing many casualties; out of a train of 200 mules which accompanied Rajputana Rifles, only 20 animals reached the forward zone. Nevertheless timing was preserved and at 2359 hours 'B' and 'C' Companies of the Rajputana Rifles scrambled forward across the scrabbly slopes in a third bid for the defiant crest of Point 593. Intense fighting followed. It was 45 minutes before the situation could be pieced together. Then it was learned that groups of gallant riflemen had gained the summit. Along the parapeted ditch reached by Lieut. Cox on the previous evening a grenade battle raged. But the main strength of the companies was held back by incessant small arms fire less than 100 yards from the final objective. At 0140 hours Lieut. Colonel Scott called for a five minutes artillery concentration on the summit; under cover of this bombardment 'D' Company swung wide and endeavoured to reach the crown of the knoll from the left flank. 90 minutes of bitter fighting followed. At 0315 hours all three forward companies reported that they were pinned down and that counter-attacks appeared to be imminent. Major Markham-Lee was missing and two other company commanders were wounded; only two British officers remained on their feet. At 0430 hours Colonel Scott sent his last company into the battle, but to no avail. On the vital half acre of shaggy crest the panzer grenadiers bared their teeth and stood like the rocks themselves.

"After the fall of Cassino the bodies of Major Markham-Lee, Jemedar Maru Ram (who was posthumously awarded the IOM) and a number of riflemen were found inside the ruined fort. They had died in the heart of the enemy defences. Rajputana Rifles casualties amounted to 196 of all ranks.

"Despite failure to win the vital Point 593 objective the battle continued according to plan. At 0215 hours, while the Rajputana Rifles strove for the crest, less than 300 yards away 1/9 Gurkha Rifles with 'A' Company in the lead advanced from 4/16 Punjabis positions, skirted the fringe of the fighting and struck downhill towards Point 444, an intervening ridge only 300 yards from the rear walls of the Monastery. As the hillmen passed through a small orchard they came under heavy converging fire from Point 593, looming quarter right, and from Point 450, a knoll 500 yards to the left, which represented the extreme flank of 7 Brigade's attack. 'A' Company's thrust line opened a gap between the Gurkhas and Rajputana Rifles; into this gap 'B' Company drove, pushing up the eastern slope of Point 593 towards Point 569, 300 yards on the left of the Rajputana Rifles' objective. Captain Arthur Bond of 'C' Company with one of his platoons joined in the rush and disappeared in the darkness. When the assault companies thinned out under the murderous fire 'D' Company threw its weight into the attack, but all to no avail. The crossfire beat the assailants into the ground and the advance was brought to a halt with the loss of 94 of all ranks.

"On the left flank, 1/2 Gurkha Rifles, also from jump-off positions in the 4/16 Punjabis sector, deployed with 'A' and 'B' Companies in the lead, their left flank resting on Point 450. At 0330 hours the hillmen began to work towards a low intermediate wrinkle of ground beyond which the slopes fell away into a hollow beneath the north walls of the Monastery. Beyond this false crest aerial photographs had shown a belt of scrub. It was impossible to reconnoitre this area, but as such undergrowth had proven negotiable elsewhere it was presumed that it did not constitute a serious obstacle. As a result the leading companies walked into a death trap. This scrub proved to be thorn thicket seeded with anti-personnel mines, its outskirts threaded with trip wires linked to booby traps. Behind this deadly barrier storm troopers lay in wait, in machine gun posts less than 50 yards apart. Between these nests foxholes sheltered enemy tommygunners and bomb throwers.

"As the Gurkhas closed up on the scrub a shower of grenades arced out of the night. Lieut. Colonel Showers' instructions had been explicit – to close on the enemy at all costs. The leading platoons dashed into the undergrowth and blew up almost to a man. Colonel Showers fell shot through the stomach. Two-thirds of the leading company was struck down within five minutes yet the survivors continued to force their way ahead. Riflemen were found afterwards with as many as four trip wires around their legs. Naik Birbahadur Thapa, although wounded in many places, managed to burst through the scrub and to seize a position in the midst of the stormtroopers. Stretcher-bearer Sherbadadur Thapa made 16 trips across this deadly ground before he was killed. An unscathed handful battled on until ordered to withdraw. Seven British officers, 4 Gurkha officers and 138 other ranks had fallen.

"After 15 minutes fighting in which both 'B' and 'C' Companies had been reduced to platoon strength, the survivors of 'C' Company under Major Ormsby, who was wounded, gained the meagre shelter of a shallow nullah. 'B' Company, under Major Raysay-Brown, was recalled to dig in behind the fatal belt of scrub. When 'A' Company came forward to reinforce the firing line, Lieut. Loftus-Tottenham, of a family of long Indian Army associations, was killed in a fearless rush at a spandau post. 'D' Company likewise closed up and began to consolidate in a position around Point 450, with Battalion Headquarters more or less in the firing line. Major G. S. N. Richardson came forward and took over command.

"Dawn broke with Rajputana Rifles, Royal Sussex and the two Gurkha battalions pinned down in front of their objectives. A little ground had been gained in the centre where 'A' and 'B' Companies of 1/9 Gurkha Rifles were embedded in the enemy's defensive system; on the right and left flanks there had been no gain. Three companies of Rajputana Rifles were astride Point 593 but withheld from the crest. Behind them, echeloned on their left flank, lay three companies of the Royal Sussex. 'C' and 'D' Companies of 1/9 Gurkhas were in touch with the Sussex on their right and with 1/2 Gurkhas on their left. The latter battalion after extrication from the death trap on their immediate front had spread to flank and 'A' and 'D' Companies now held Point 445, 300 yards on the left of Point 450 and approximately 500 yards from the north-east corner of the Monastery Walls. With the recall of the two forward companies of 1/9 Gurkhas 7 Brigade stood almost in its original jump-off positions. No ground had been gained, no hole had been punched in the defences. Within bowshot the battered Monastery walls towered, aloof and impregnable."

*   *   *   *   *

On the Hill with 4/16 Punjabis

When we took over at Cassino from the Americans the Battalion area was strewn with American dead, and we were instructed not to bury them. In addition, the carcases of hundreds of mules were rotting everywhere. But for the intense cold and snow, disease would soon have spread; as it was we were all covered in lice within a few days.

Our forward positions were along a ridge to the north of, and overlooked by, the Monastery. So close were we to the German positions that we could hear them talking.

Rations were brought up at night. One night, "B" Company CQMH missed the company position and by-passed it. His party by some miracle went through the German lined unchallenged! On hearing some movement the party, realising their mistake, lay very still, and then a German mortar detachment set up its mortars by them. The detachment went on firing until dawn when it packed up and went away. By this time it was getting light and the ration party couldn't move. It lay still throughout the whole day. In the afternoon they suffered, with the Germans, an intense aerial and artillery bombardment. When night fell they crept back undetected and so we got our rations: one day late and very cold!

In none of the official accounts is it mentioned that our forward positions were inside the "bomb-line" and what was meant for the Germans was meant for us too. This was no error of judgement – it just had to be as we were so close to each other and the Monastery. There could be no movement during the day and we all suffered severely from cramp in the limbs.

A further hazard was the now famous Cassino artillery smoke screen our gunners laid to cover the movement of other troops in the Liri valley and who were overlooked by the monastery OPs. This smoke screen continued, as far as I can remember, for some weeks – even at night when the moon was bright. When the wind blew from the north the smoke shells had to be fired on to our positions. As a result of the bombing and smoke shells were suffered many casualties.

There was an unwritten "gentleman's agreement" with the Germans regarding the evacuation of wounded. When a man was wounded a red flag was raised by whichever side suffered the casualty. All firing ceased in that area and spotters in the rear, seeing the red flag would come forward with stretchers.

When the stretcher party had returned with its load the flag would be lowered and firing and mortaring would begin again until the next casualty.

"A" Company went into Cassino 110 plus strong, but when the time came to leave, in spite of reinforcements, we left with only 33 men. It was much the same in the other Companies.

* * * * *

"Surgical Spirit"

For the infantry Cassino was the supreme ordeal. What it might have been if the medical services had not risen to the challenge must remain to the imagination. In six weeks more than 4,000 men of 4th Indian Division were killed or wounded. To cope with this overwhelming emergency, Colonel R. L. Raymond, ADMS, who had replaced Colonel F. R. H. Mollan, OBE MC, on the latter's retirement at the end of 1943, brought 17 Field Ambulance (Lieut-Colonel H. J. R. Thorne, DSO, RAMC), 26 Field Ambulance (Lieut-Colonel G. S. N. Hughes, DSO, IMS), 32 Field Ambulance (Lieut-Colonel C. W. Green, IMS), which had arrived with 11 Brigade, and 2 Indian Mobile Casualty Clearing Station (Lieut-Colonel C. Reed, RAMC), together with a group of volunteer ambulances of American Field Service, onto the battlefield. Whether from the crests behind the Monastery or from the mountainside below it, or from the Rapido valley, the rescue, evacuation and care of casualties proceeded in full view of the enemy. Many British and Indian soldiers are alive to-day because no danger was sufficient to deter the devoted stretcher-bearers, doctors and orderlies from their day and night struggle against imminent death.

7 Brigade's opening assault along the bare fire-swept summits in the rear of the Monastery imposed a severe strain on the medical units. Captain E. Bowmer, 17 Field Ambulance, organised the evacuation route down the hillside. Many officers and men owe their lives to this gallant doctor. A motor ambulance Car Head and an advanced dressing station under Captain Minford was established in the ruins of Cairo village. For several miles to the rear the road was under fire. A medical officer who traversed this track daily paid a tribute to the American Field Ambulance which was equally applicable to all ambulance drivers:

"The river crossing – Windy Corner – received an unhealthy amount of shelling. Jeeps did not tarry there. Yet in full daylight, an American volunteer halted his ambulance, rescued a wounded man, dressed his wounds, took him to the advanced dressing station under continuous fire, and classified it as 'all in the day's work'. Another driver lost his ambulance when a near miss ditched it, but continued on foot and brought in four Indians under a hail of fire. Day and night, and non-stop if necessary, these American boys would carry on. They could always be trusted to get through, no matter how sticky the situation."

From the advanced dressing station jeep ambulances negotiated a rough and difficult mountain track for nearly a mile along the slopes of the massif. At "Ambulance Jeep Head", Captain Aslam, IMS, operated a forward dressing station. Here, during the early fighting, 16 stretcher-bearers were knocked out by a single shell. Thence a steep, narrow and winding mule path continued for 2 miles towards Point 593 where the most advanced dressing station was set up by Captain Bhatia and Captain Ghaznavi (26 Field Ambulance) in conjunction with regimental aid posts of Royal Sussex (Captain Reilly), 1/6 Rajputana Rifles (Captain Karney), 1/2 Gurkhas (Captain Jones) and 1/9 Gurkhas (Captain Sonnic). These casualty assembly points, possessing only the sparse cover afforded by a bleak mountainside, received a full measure of attention from the enemy. The Royal Sussex and 1/9 Gurkha posts were hit no less than 15 times by mortar of shell fire.

The hand-carry route for casualties therefore covered a distance of nearly 4 miles. While ambulance mules with litters and cacolets were available, the steepness and slipperiness of the slopes and the danger of animals stampeding under shell fire, prevented their use. Four-hundred stretcher-bearers, ambulance and jeep drivers were constantly moving up and down in the service of the wounded. Lieut-Colonel G. S. N. Hughes DSO, was in command; his abounding energy and unfailing resource surmounted every difficulty. The medical units were reinforced by a flow of volunteer stretcher-bearers – from 57 LAA Regiment, 149 Anti-Tank Regiment, from the pioneer companies, even from the followers. Baz Mir, a dhobi, won the IDSM for repeated trips to Hangman's Hill. Sepoy Chet Singh, a jeep driver from 4/16 Punjabis, covered the route to the Rapido more than 100 times. Mortally wounded, he died while helping a wounded comrade to safety. Towards the end of the battle when the ranks of the Battalion stretcher-bearers had been depleted by casualties, groups from the advanced dressing stations went forward to search the forward lines and to bring in the wounded from where they fell.

Between the first and the second battles casualties continued at the rate of nearly 100 daily. When 5 Brigade entered the battle in the castle area, the work of the medical services doubled, since there was no diminution in the flow of wounded from the crests behind the monastery. (In the first two days of fighting, 5 Brigade evacuated 213 casualties; in its static section 7 Brigade lost 150 men.) 26 Field Ambulance set up an advanced dressing station at the foot of Castle Hill, and sent its groups scouring forward to find and to fetch in the stricken. Naik Mohammed Yusef IOM IDSM, organised the evacuation of the wounded along a track continuously under shell fire. He was afterwards presented to the King-Emperor, who complimented him on his courage. Lance-Naik Maiappa Ral, after being buried for six hours in debris on the edge of Cassino town, continued on duty for five days and repeatedly braved German snipers to rescue men who had fallen in the open. The battle evolved into a mêlée in which some of the medical personnel saw even more of the enemy than did the fighting troops. On 18th March Captain Sonnic and Captain Bhatia sallied from the castle with their stretcher-bearers in broad daylight to bring in 24 wounded from the lower hairpin bend. Encountering the enemy, they were allowed to pass, one officer being detained as hostage. Thereafter stretcher-bearers were permitted to proceed on similar errands of mercy, but only in small groups. Sergeant Roche of 26 Field Ambulance led a party to Hangman's Hill, bringing in 30 wounded and taking back first-aid supplies and blood plasma. The garrison of Hangman's Hill was under medical charge of Lance-Corporal Edmond Hazle DCM, of 1/4 Essex, who with Lance-Corporal Leonard Piper of the same battalion, handled upwards of 200 casualties in the eight days of isolation. Major operations and even amputations were performed by Hazle from the slender resources of his first-aid haversack. To bring the wounded down the precipitous and slippery slopes, avoiding the mined footways, it was necessary to rope sling from one foothold to another, with the wounded tied to the stretchers by fish netting.

At the main dressing station, in a nullah near San Michele, the Indian units were supplemented by 28 British Field Surgical Unit, 6 New Zealand Field Surgical Unit and a blood transfusion team. Here the long suffering and exhausted casualties found beds, if only briefly before evacuation. Yet even here there was no safety. On 16th March the area was systematically shelled. Casualties to medical personnel included Captain Seth, whose arm was severed while he attended a patient. 32 Field Ambulance, less companies on forward evacuation, operated a main dressing station at

Piedmonte d'Alife, from which the wounded flowed to 2 Indian Mobile Casualty Clearing Station at Pressenzano.

It is impossible in the space available to give individual credit to all who met and triumphantly encompassed the greatest medical emergency in Divisional history. As all shared the dangers, so all earned the bays.

At Cassino 4th Indian Division lost more than a battle. It lost some of its very substance in the form of the men who had moulded it.

*   *   *   *   *

"User Trials"

There is a time lapse between physical and mental involvement in outside events and the transfer of concentration to happenings to one's body. There is a surprising vagueness sometimes; a reluctance, almost amounting to lethargy, to do something about it. The fact and the extent of the damage is sometimes clearer to others.

Sending a message back was initiated but did it happen? The mist begins to thicken. The OP team are still there. He is with them in the Jeep: he does not know how. It is a long way back and it is a rough ride.

There is a pause, at a guess, at a Regimental Aid Post. Where? Who knows? but it seems very quiet; tucked somewhere into a hill in the lower slopes. Then there is nothing.

*   *   *   *   *

Vague pictures of blood in bottles come into focus, and then there is a bright picture of lucidity. This must be an Advanced Dressing Station somewhere. It seems to be night. There is a space and a number of people: also a discussion. What is the best way to get him to the rear? Priority on the route is for armour and other traffic moving forward. The tracks are in an appalling state. Would it be better to continue to use a Jeep-mounted stretcher in the hope that the smaller vehicle could get through, or an American covered ambulance, with less good cross-country ability but more comfort and weather protection if things went wrong? Rather unexpectedly, he joins in, with a very firm casting vote for the latter. The journey seems to go on for a long, long, time. At least, whenever there is awareness of surroundings this is the protective shield of the ambulance; sometimes halted, sometimes lurching along.

*   *   *.   *   *

When the mist clears finally, the tent turns out to be one of several in a Main Dressing Station with Field Surgical Units attached (it proved to be in a dry "torrente" bed near San Michele). It seems to be within the 100% zone (sometimes, it seemed the 50% zone) of several German guns. There are better places to be when being shelled than immobile, with numerous tubes attached, on a bed in a tent!

c

* * * * *

The best condition to be in then is to be unconscious. But the morphine administered during the earlier, more painful phases – takes less and less effect. The splendid surgeon was as skilled in psychology. To assist sleep, what about a personal bottle of Scotch within reach? (The ration of Scotch over on the Adriatic side at Christmas had been missed, and Canadian rye had been no substitute.) It beats morphine into a cocked hat.

* * * * *

The only common denominator in that tent is that all the patients are "heads or stomachs", none are able to be evacuated farther back to the Casualty Clearing Station until they have been operated upon and then recovered sufficiently to make movement safe; or until they have accompanied the mortuary Sergeant on his late nightly quest of "Anything for me?". The recovery rate is astonishingly high; particularly bearing in mind the conditions. Two obstacles that splendid staff cannot overcome are the effects of being too long before being attended to (and on the peaks and slopes around Cassino this was often unavoidable), and patients' failure to co-operate.

Two patients in the latter category are a Free French Officer who makes frequent wild sorties up and down the aisle between beds, with tubes flying (because they are still connected to him, but pulled out of their reservoirs), and one or more wine bottles in his hand. He seemed to enjoy this, but it proves to be a short-sighted policy. The other is an Italian muleteer, who is apparently convinced that all this tube business, injections etc. are malevolent. He always pulls out everything and eventually, and inevitably, this includes the plug of his own life.

* * * * *

It is a wonderful place to see how differently the various races react to pain. There are many Indian races, New Zealanders, British, French, Moroccan, and Italian. Never has the silent stoicism of the Gurkha been more apparent: a real obstacle in some cases to easy diagnosis.

The efforts of the Indian Field Ambulance cookhouse to provide from their rations appetising and digestable food for such awkward and defective stomachs are remarkable.

The results achieved by the co-operation between races under appalling difficulties in that ADS/FST group are incredible and beyond praise.

* * * * *

Aftermath

For 4th Indian Division as for many other fine divisions, Cassino was a Gethsemane. Here passed the last of the old hands and few of those who joined the Division for the first time in Europe could really understand what superb standards had hitherto been the norm. Withdrawn to the Adriatic Coast the Division entered an unpleasant sector and gradually took over a wide front. The breakthrough on the Rapido in April led to an enemy withdrawal. Early in June the Division was briefed for pursuit and followed up the retreat, mopping up rearguards and liberating Chieti, Pescara and Citta San Angelo. In this advance 149th Anti-Tank Regiment distinguished itself by the speed with which it overcame obstacles and kept its screen ahead of the rapidly moving infantry. After relief by the Poles, the Division returned to Campobasso for training. A trek into Central Italy followed, for the Germans after the loss of Rome were ending their long retreat in the mountainus terrain between Lake Trasimeno and the Tiber. Here on 8th July, with 10th Brigade of 10th Indian Division under command, 4th Indian Division joined in the arduous process of prying the Germans from their grip on the serried ridges between the valleys of the Arno and the Tiber.

Another King George Sees the Action

After returning to the front in mid-July 1944, 4th Indian Division relieved 2nd New Zealand Division in the Arezzo area, with 11th Infantry Brigade holding the area to the north of Arezzo. 3/12 Frontier Force was ordered to capture the high Campiano feature five miles to the north and clearly visible from Arezzo itself.

The attack was launched at 1700 hours on 25th July. It was on a two-company front and was supported by a squadron of tanks from the Royal Warwickshire Yeomanry, a battery from 11th Field Regiment and a battery from 5th Medium Regiment.

By last light the right forward company had run into trouble and suffered heavy casualties. A number of tanks had also been lost. Help was called for and a company from 2/7 Gurkhas was sent forward to reinforce the position.

The left forward company succeeded in continuing its advance, capturing several enemy posts and, in the light of this success, the reserve company was pushed through up the hill to make the final assault. However, about three-quarters of the way up the hill, and at about 0200 hours, the company encountered a thick minefield and took several casualties. The Battalion commander decided that in view of the casualties in men and tanks, and the loss of momentum, the companies should dig in, hold on to their gains and be prepared to advance on the following evening.

Colonel McDonald, the Battalion Commander, was telephoned by the Brigade Commander at 0900 hours and asked what his plan was for that day. The CO said that he would launch his attack with two companies up the spur on his left flank, supported by fire from the Gurkha company on the right. The attack, which was to start at 1700 hours, would be made under cover of a smoke screen from his mortars, the two artillery batteries, and the six remaining tanks. The Brigadier accepted the plan, and said that the code-word for the attack would be "David's in the Chair". The unusual nature of the code-word passed unnoticed amongst the CO and his staff in the general fatigue and strain of the action.

The smoke barrage duly came down and the attack started but to the Battalion's amazement the whole Campriano feature was enveloped in smoke and disappeared in a barrage which had obviously been fired by considerably more weapons than the Battalion Commander had at his disposal. When the barrage stopped and the leading platoons were nearing the summit an Italian priest came running down the slope shouting, "The

Tedesci have gone," and so they had. The hill was taken with a loss, during the battle, of 25 killed and 70 wounded.

The following day the purport of "David's in the Chair" was made clear to the Battalion Commanders. His Majesty King George VI had watched the action from the steps of the citadel at Arezzo (where he also subsequently presented medals to members of the Division). It must have been an impressive spectacle. The Divisional Artillery, and almost certainly some from Corps, had joined in and the 3/12 and the rest of the Division will always remember that boost that His Majesty gave them that evening from Arezzo.

As far as is known, this was the first occasion that King George VI had watched an action in the Second World War. In doing so he was following an example set by a King George 200 years before at Dettingen.

* * * * *

More Majorum

Not the least of the remarkable qualities of 4th Indian Division was its powers of recovery. There was no doubt that the losses at Cassino had been dire. In attempting the impossible once too often the Division had been sorely wounded. "Jo Hukm" had almost been a last testament: almost, but not quite. As the Divisional history records:

"General Holworthy had taken over Fourth Indian Division when it was still shaken by the tragedy of Cassino. Fortune was kind and his men were vouchsafed the opportunity to regain their wonted dash and resilience in a series of operations of rising severity."

There can be no better illustration of this than the description in the History of an attack by 1/2 Gurkhas during Operation VANDAL.

"Moving by night and in silence, 1/2 Gurkhas before dawn on July 20th had secured Point 684 in the centre of the Piane di Maggio hogsback. During the forenoon a company seized Point 775, 1,000 yards to the north-west. This sudden incursion with its double threat to Verazzano took the enemy by surprise but rallying quickly German troops threw in a succession of heavy assaults in an effort to regain the lost ground. Throughout the afternoon counter-attacks followed in quick succession. The thick scrub and fir groves enabled the enemy to concentrate close to the Gurkha positions. The defenders would have been critically placed had it not been for the magnificent work of 31

Field Regiment and the support of the Wiltshire Yeomanry's Shermans. The gunners fired 800 rounds, the tanks 450 rounds. Never since Garci did artillery deal with enemy threats in such summary fashion. In spite of heavy and continuous mortar fire the Gurkhas managed during the afternoon to extend their gains. A swift pounce afterwards described by the Corps Commander as 'brilliantly successful' carried Major the Hon. L. C. F. Shore and his company to a further objective. Unfortunately this officer, whose family connection with his regiment began in the first campaign 135 years before, was mortally wounded. The day's fighting cost the Gurkhas substantial casualties and the Germans left 60 dead on the ground."

The Division's part in the bitter battle for the Gothic Line was described by the Divisional History briefly, but graphically, as follows:

"It was now 37 days since Fourth Indian Division had moved out of Sigillo and 32 days since it had opened the battle. In this period the three brigades had advanced more than 60 miles, of which the last 25 miles had been in constant contact with a desperately resisting enemy. Casualties had been heavy, amounting to 1,892 of all ranks, including an unusually high percentage of junior officers. The average strength of companies was now less than 30 rifles. The battle had been of the most wearing type – no set piece assaults on the grand scale with intimate preparation and subsequent relief, but an unrelenting series of small bitter clashes for each acre of gained or lost ground. Companies seized limited objectives; other companies passed through to register gains or to be flung back; the enemy fought with frenzy throughout the hours of darkness to be gone at dawn – but only as far as the next crest behind. Always a dominating ridge barred the way; when won, a swollen stream curtained by mortar fire lay behind it. To advance up a fire-swept hillside, surge over the crest, descend the reverse slopes in full view of the enemy, pick paths across deadly mined ground along the river banks, splash through icy torrents scarcely colder than the pelting rains, work up another slope against another crest stiff with enemies; with support arms, sappers, medicals and supply services following up; battling by night and day against abominable terrain and foul winter weather – such was the recurrent log of Fourth Indian Division's five week's drive along the Apennine foothills.

"It had been felt and said – sadly by friends, casually by others – that Fourth Indian Division had been destroyed at Cassino and never would be the same again. To this opinion the Gothic Line battle supplied abundant and eloquent refutation. The record of this operation is rich in characteristic performances by all ranks of the Division – great courage in extremity, indomitable doggedness, quick improvisation, the ability to make war and to win through against every stress of circumstance. The new units bore themselves with the same pride and resolution as their predecessors."

At Lake Trasimeno in north Italy, 4th Indian Division's campaign in Italy, which had started on 8th Army's front on the Gustav line on the Ortona–Orsogna highway, came to an honourable close when it was ordered to Greece and a very different task: that of peace-keeping in a country torn by civil war – different, but testing to the last.

*   *   *   *   *

Peace-keeping in Greece

A short account from 1/4th Essex *by Major (then) Denis Beckett* DSO, *describes a typical situation in the confused fighting which the Division found in Greece.*

"The ELAS Commander disposed of about 75,000 troops in Athens and Piraeus. They were well equipped with automatics and rifles, and in addition possessed a number of mortars and field guns of German and Italian origin. By December 9th, when the Battalion commenced operations in the Piraeus, only the fringes of the docks were held by a small British Force, pitifully thin upon the ground. The guerillas had the enormous advantage of knowing the town, and only a few wore any kind of uniform, so could always mingle with the ordinary civilians if forced into a tight corner.

"Still they were sometimes tough fighters, and attempts to enter buildings without heavy fire support almost always drew showers of grenades upon the attackers. On one occasion, after a fierce struggle the remnants of a force holding a bank attempted to escape in a captured ambulance still bearing the Red Cross. In fact, their attitude to the Red Cross was a bit peculiar, to say the least. On another occasion, when some tanks returned fire on a hospital from which enemy snipers had been active, a small group of guerillas appeared on the balcony, and in an attitude of magnificent defiance, hurled home-made bombs at our armour with small Red Cross flags attached to them.

"But less amusing was the morning after we had broken up an enemy attack to find among the dead the body of a nurse. She was fully armed and carrying ammunition. Such incidents were rare, but it gives some indication of the bitter nature of the fighting. And as the guerillas were not above using women and small children to carry fresh supplies of ammunition for them the problems of the soldiers trying to fight with care for the innocent became terrific.

"However, experience and fire power were on our side, and two days of fighting sufficed to seal off an area enabling the remainder of the Brigade to undertake a successful sweeping operation which cleared the whole of the eastern side of the harbour. Then on the night of December 21st–22nd, we landed on the opposite side of the docks, and in hard fighting drove the enemy back to the outer edges of the town. At first we obtained a certain amount of tactical surprise, but within 48 hours he began to react violently and counter-attacked with mortar and artillery support. His efforts availed him nothing, and on Christmas Day, C Coy, stormed the Papastratos Cigarette Factory, a very large block in the north of the town, and after half-an-hour's bombardment by tanks, mortars and machine guns, forced the surrender of the garrison at a cost of only one casualty to themselves. They took 300 prisoners and much booty, including a large quantity of machine guns and explosives.

"Most of the fighting took place in densely-populated districts, where care of the civilians was added to the usual problems. Apart from fighting a battle, the slender resources of Battalion organisation were stretched to include a system for dealing with evacuees. For several days the cooks fed over 500 civilians from our own resources. And for the medical staff there was always the chance of an outbreak of some epidemic among the thousands of dehoused persons sheltering in the basements of factories and warehouses."

Valete

As a last contribution to this book it seems fitting to reproduce the valediction from someone who contributed so much to 4th Indian Division, its commander from January 1942 to March 1944, the late Lieutenant-General Sir Francis Tuker KCIE CB DSO OBE. In his farewell message to the Division, he wrote:

"For two years and a quarter it has been my good fortune to serve with you. Now the time has come for me to go. I can never forget you.

"You have built a brotherhood in arms such as has seldom been equalled in our long history.

"Your great battles are carved deep on the tablets of this war. I have never known you falter. I have only seen your courage, your tenacity and the skill and fierceness of your attack, that has won you victories which have astonished the rest of the Army.

"May God speed you and bear you with good cheer and hope through every test which lies before you to the final Victory."